MURTY CLASSICAL
LIBRARY OF INDIA

NANDI TIMMANA
THEFT OF A TREE

NANDI TIMMANA

THEFT
OF A TREE

A Tale by the Court Poet of the
Vijayanagara Empire

Translated by

HARSHITA MRUTHINTI KAMATH
and **VELCHERU NARAYANA RAO**

MURTY CLASSICAL LIBRARY OF INDIA
HARVARD UNIVERSITY PRESS
Cambridge, Massachusetts
London, England
2024

First published in Murty Classical Library of India,
Volume 32, Harvard University Press, 2022.

SERIES DESIGN BY M9DESIGN

Library of Congress Cataloging-in-Publication Data

Names: Nandi Timmana, active 16th century, author. |
Kamath, Harshita Mruthinti, 1982- translator. |
Narayana Rao, Velcheru, 1932- translator. |
Nandi Timmana, active 16th century. Pārijātāpaharaṇamu. |
Nandi Timmana, active 16th century. Pārijātāpaharaṇamu. English.
Title: Theft of a tree / Nandi Timmana ;
translated by Harshita Mruthinti Kamath
and Velcheru Narayana Rao.
Other titles: Murty classical library of India ; 32.
Description: Cambridge, Massachusetts :
Harvard University Press, 2022. |
Series: Murty classical library of India; 32 |
Includes bibliographical references. | Introduction and
notes in English followed by translations of poems |
Identifiers: LCCN 2021010032 |
ISBN 9780674295919 (pbk.)
Subjects: LCSH: Krishna (Hindu deity)--Poetry.
Classification: LCC PL4780.9.N294 P313 2022 |
DDC 894.8/2712--dc23
LC record available at https://lccn.loc.gov/2021010032

CONTENTS

INTRODUCTION

The story of Krishna's theft of the *pārijāta*—the divine, flowering tree that grants all desires—from Indra's garden to please his favorite wife, Satyabhama, has been immensely popular in Telugu literary and performance traditions for centuries and has taken on a life of its own in a manner similar to retellings of the Ramayana.[1] The widespread popularity of the narrative in Telugu begins with Nandi Timmana's epic poem *Pārijātāpaharaṇamu* (Theft of a Tree), written at the height of the classical Telugu literary tradition at the court of Krishnadevaraya (r. 1509–1529), the most powerful among the rulers of the Vijayanagara empire (c. 1346–1565).

Divided across five chapters *Theft of a Tree* opens with a customary frame narrative, in which King Janamejaya asks the sage Vaishampayana to relate the story of Krishna's theft of the *pārijāta* tree.

The sage tells the tale as follows: One day, while Krishna is spending time with his chief queen Rukmini, the sage Narada visits him on earth, in the town of Dvaraka. Narada gives Krishna a single *pārijāta* flower from Indra's garden in heaven, which Krishna gifts to Rukmini. Krishna's beloved wife Satyabhama comes to learn of the *pārijāta* gift from her maid, and she immediately retires to her anger chamber (*kopasadana*), her pride deeply hurt. Finding his favorite wife in a distraught state, Krishna promises Satyabhama that he will bring her the entire *pāri-*

jāta tree from Indra's garden. He journeys with her to Indra's garden in heaven and uproots the tree. After an epic battle with Indra, Krishna steals the tree, brings it to earth, and plants it in Satyabhama's garden. Satyabhama then performs the *puṇyaka vrata,* a votive rite in which she is required to give away the tree and her husband to the sage Narada. The story ends with Krishna living in endless happiness with Satyabhama and his other wives.

The Author

According to one of the most popular and enduring legends of the Vijayanagara period, King Krishnadevaraya is said to have hosted eight different poets in the eight corners of his illustrious hall, Bhuvanavijaya (Conquest of the World). Seated in the center of this hall, Krishnadevaraya is thought to have enjoyed the literary discourses of these eight poets, who were known as the *aṣṭadiggajālu,* the Eight Elephants who bear the burden of the earth. While this legend cannot be historically verified, one thing we know for certain is that Nandi Timmana, along with his contemporary, Allasani Peddana, were two poets present in Krishnadevaraya's court.[2]

What little we do know about Timmana comes from a single verse at the end of the fifth chapter of *Theft of a Tree,* in which the author, referring to himself as "Timmaya," tells us something about his own biography:

Timmaya
of the Kaushika clan and Apastambha lineage

in the flawless Six Thousand Family,
son of Nandi Singana and Timmamba,
wise with learning,
nephew of the poet honored as "Cool Breeze from
    Malaya Mountain,"
feted by King Krishnaraya with palanquins and gifts of
    villages,
his mind focused on Shiva,
disciple of Aghorashivaguru,
composed this Telugu poem, Theft of a Tree,
to last as long as the sun, stars, and moon.[3]

The unusual location of this verse in Timmana's text is itself
interesting. In most classical Telugu poems, starting with
Nannaya's epic in the eleventh century, the poet begins his
literary work by setting forth the context in which his poem
came to be composed. For instance, Timmana's contempo-
rary, Peddana, elaborately describes the courtly scene in
which his poem, *Manucaritramu* (The Story of Manu), was
commissioned. Seated in his illustrious hall, King Krishnade-
varaya praises Peddana for his skill with words and requests
him to write a poem about the life of Manu.[4] This prelude
resembles the opening verses of Nannaya's *Mahābhārat-*
amu, which is considered to be the very first text of clas-
sical Telugu literature. Just as Krishnadevaraya requests
that Peddana compose *Manucaritramu,* the eleventh-cen-
tury king Rajarajanarendra asks Nannaya to compose the
Sanskrit *Mahābhārata* in Telugu.[5] All of this is missing in
Theft of a Tree, which begins with no mention of the context
in which the poem came to be commissioned. Instead, we

find a lone autobiographical verse at the very end of the fifth chapter. This noticeable absence of context has led commentators to suggest that Krishnadevaraya may not have directly commissioned Timmana to write this epic poem.

While we may never know the actual circumstances of the composition of Timmana's text, later Telugu literary tradition provides us with a remarkable reason. According to popular legend, Timmana is said to have arrived in Krishnadevaraya's court as a marital gift from the family of Tirumaladevi, the senior wife of the king. One night, Krishnadevaraya awoke to find his wife sleeping by his side with her feet in his face. He became upset by her lack of respect and stopped speaking to her for a long time. Timmana, according to the legend, composed *Theft of a Tree* on behalf of the queen, who sought to win back her husband's affections.[6]

Mirroring this interaction, Timmana's narrative prominently describes how Satyabhama kicks Krishna, who then lovingly forgives her. This detail is markedly absent from any other *pārijāta* narrative, either in Sanskrit or in other vernacular languages. Satyabhama's kick appears in two of the most popular verses in the first chapter:

He saw no way to appease the anger in her heart.
Nothing was working.
Krishna, master puppeteer who pulls the strings of
    the world,
bowed down to her feet, soft as the lotus,
their redness heightening the radiance of his jeweled
    crown.

She kicked him with her left foot,
right on the head—
a head worthy of worship by Brahma and Indra,
the head of the father of the love god.
That's how it is.

When a husband crosses the line,
does an angry wife know what she's doing?[7]

These verses seemingly serve as a message to Krishnade-
varaya: if Krishna himself submits and even enjoys a kick
from the left foot of his beloved wife, the king should not be
angered by the feet of his wife at his head. The connection
between Krishnadevaraya and Krishna is underscored in
the opening section of Timmana's poem, in which the poet
describes King Krishnadevaraya as the very incarnation of
the god Krishna: "Krishna came back as Krishnaraya, god
himself in human form."[8]

Another popular legend about Timmana features his
sobriquet, Mukku Timmana, or "Timmana of the Nose."
Timmana is said to have written the following verse about
a beautiful woman's nose, which, in Telugu and Sanskrit
convention, is compared to a *campaka* flower:

In agony, the *campaka* blossom wondered
why bees enjoy the honey of so many flowers
but never come to her.
She fled to the forest to do penance.
As a reward, she achieved the shape of a woman's
    nose.

Now she takes in the perfumes
of all the flowers, and on both sides
she is honored by eyes
black as bees.[9]

The legend goes on to explain that Bhattumurti, also known as Ramarajabhushana, bought this verse from Timmana and included it in his poem, *Vasucaritramu*. While it is doubtful that Timmana and Bhattumurti even lived at the same time, this legend, almost certainly from a later period, demonstrates the imagined world of intertextuality between Telugu poets and the interesting mercantile value of a verse that could be bought and sold.[10] Although the biography of Timmana remains limited to a single verse, the contribution of his literary work extends far beyond the reaches of his text. As an actual poet in Krishnadevaraya's court, and a poet included in the imagined *aṣṭadiggajālu*, Timmana participated in a sixteenth-century south Indian literary and courtly milieu that conflated the figures of god and king and reimagined the relationships of the human and divine.

Nandi Timmana and Classical Telugu Literature

The narrative of Krishna's theft of the *pārijāta* tree from Indra's garden does not begin with Timmana's *Pārijātāpaharaṇamu* but, rather, has permeated Indian literatures for more than a millennium. The earliest reference to the *pārijāta* episode is found in the Sanskrit *Harivaṁśa*, which is considered to be an appendix to the *Mahābhārata*.[11] The *pāri-*

jāta episode is also present in Puranic texts, including *Viṣṇu Purāṇa* (ca. early centuries C.E.).[12] The theme is elaborated upon in later Sanskrit texts, such as the *Pārijātāharaṇa* of Umapatidhara (twelfth century) and the *Pārijātāharaṇa* by Kavikarnapura (sixteenth century).[13] The *Harivijaya,* a Maharashtri Prakrit text by Sarvasena (fifth century; extant today only in fragments), is perhaps the earliest non-Sanskrit elaboration on the *pārijāta* theme.[14] The episode also appears in other regional languages, including Rudrabhatta's Kannada text *Jagannāthavijaya* (thirteenth century), the *Sāralā Mahābhārata* from Orissa (fifteenth century), and Shankaradeva's Maithili drama *Pārijātāharaṇa* (sixteenth century).[15]

Given the widespread appearance of the *pārijāta* episode across Sanskrit and vernacular literatures, Timmana's focus on this theme might appear unremarkable. The questions of who borrowed from whom and which version of the *pārijāta* theme is earliest are beyond the scope of this short introduction. What is important for us here is not the historical question of source but, rather, how Timmana converts this narrative into an expressive poem that is uniquely situated in a Telugu landscape. As the modern Telugu poet Viswanath Satyanarayana has said:

> Ninety percent of what makes a poem
> is the genius of the poet. Poets in India know
> that the way you tell the tale
> weighs a thousand times more
> than some facile, novel theme.[16]

Classified in the poetic genre of *mahāprabandha* (great composition), *Theft of a Tree* is arguably the first Telugu literary work to adhere to a single plot. While both Sanskrit and Telugu literary texts are known for producing complex webs of interlocking, embedded narratives, Timmana departs from this practice by focusing on only the *pārijāta* story for the entirety of his poem. As a single narrative, Timmana's poem bears nascent resemblance to the modern novel in Telugu, which fully takes shape with Pingali Suranna's *Kaḷāpūrṇodayamu* a few decades later.[17] Timmana's adherence to a single plot enables him to develop his central theme, which is to elaborate upon two ways of reaching god. The first is to know Krishna to be god in the process of praising him as such. The second is to envision Krishna as purely human and fall in love with him. The characters of Timmana's poem can be thus divided into two groups: those who know Krishna to be god and those who think of Krishna as a human being. Narada, Aditi, and the poet himself envision Krishna as god, while Satyabhama sees Krishna as entirely her human husband.

Accordingly, Timmana develops two kinds of literary styles: the devotional and the aesthetic. The first literary style is present in Narada's extended praise of Krishna in the opening chapter, Aditi's tribute to Krishna in the *daṇḍaka* (garland verse) in the third chapter, and Narada's praise of Krishna in the *bandhakāvya* (binding verse) at the end of the narrative. In chapter 1, Narada's elaborate eulogy of Krishna and his ten incarnations establishes an intense devotional mood that frames the beginning of the narrative.[18] It is noteworthy that Krishna, who knows himself to be god, does not acknowledge Narada's words and, instead, speaks to him as a human being respectful of a sage. In chapter 3, Aditi also lavishes praise on Krishna in an extended devotional interlude written as a *daṇḍaka*, which is a specific genre of dynamic speech intended to be read at a fast pace with no pauses.[19] This genre is favored by Telugu poets to express a mood of intense devotion.[20] Timmana also employs *bandhakāvya*, a style of writing in which a poem imitates a picture that is generally referred to as *citrakāvya* (figural poetry) in Indian literature. He appears to be the first Telugu poet to use *bandhakāvya*, although figural poetry is present in Sanskrit centuries earlier, and his use of binding verses extends the devotional literary style of Theft of a Tree.[21] Finally, whenever we hear the poet speak in his own voice, it is clear that he knows Krishna to be god.[22]

The Narrative of Theft of a Tree

Apart from these devotional parts of the poem that envision Krishna as god, the bulk of *Theft of a Tree* is a human drama of love between Krishna and his favorite wife Satyabhama. For Satyabhama, Krishna is a human being, and she herself is a woman. The relationship between them gives the poet an extensive opportunity to describe love in all of its phases, unfolding from the very opening verses of the first chapter. When offered the *pārijāta* flower by Narada, Krishna, like a conflicted human being, worries about which wife should receive the flower as a gift: his beloved wife Satyabhama or his chief queen Rukmini, who happens to be with him at the time. Narada enhances the intensity of the play of emotions by describing, within earshot of Satyabhama's friend, the effects of the flower. Narada, who knows Krishna as god, participates fully in the human drama by stoking the rivalry between Rukmini and Satyabhama. Narada's role here, as elsewhere in Indian literature, is to create a rivalry in order to provoke action and, in the process, allow the characters to undergo an internal transformation through the course of the narrative.

Narada describes the intimate encounter between Krishna and Rukmini by explicitly stating how the flower will enhance their lovemaking.[23] Narada continues by telling Rukmini how beautiful she looks after wearing the flower and even proclaims that she will rule over all of Krishna's other wives. He mischievously incites the rivalry between co-wives by bringing Satyabhama into the conversation.[24] The spark of jealousy is now ignited by the carefully planted words of the sage, who delights in quarrels. Upon hearing the news of the *parijata* gift from her friend who witnessed it at Rukmini's palace, Satyabhama reacts "like a wounded snake ready to strike."[25] The importance Timmana gives to Satyabhama is significant here; she is always in Krishna's mind, even when he is actually giving the flower to Rukmini. Krishna worries about Satyabhama, acutely aware that she will be upset. After bidding Narada farewell, Krishna rushes off to Satyabhama's palace, his mind reeling.[26] The human drama is carried forward when Krishna finds Satyabhama in her anger chamber and falls at her feet, begging her forgiveness. Her anger climaxes at this moment, and she kicks him on the head with her left foot.

This kick to Krishna's head, described by the poet as worthy of worship by the gods, including Brahma and Indra, clearly establishes the aesthetic tone and human drama of Timmana's text.[27]

The second chapter, which features the beauty of life on earth, continues the human focus of the poem. Careful attention is paid to mundane activities such as Krishna's bath and the setting of the sun. For example, one verse describes in detail the different kinds of food that Narada and Krishna enjoy during their dinner.[28] The same enjoyment of food is extended to the moonlight feast of the *cakora* birds, as if they are human as well.[29] The beauties of moonlight are described in the second chapter in a long, intensely poetic passage, which a traditional commentator refers to as *věnnělavacanamu,* moonlight words.[30]

By the end of the second chapter, Krishna and Satyabhama mount Garuda and set off for Vaijayanta, Indra's palace, which is situated on the peak of Mount Meru. As they fly to the top of Meru, Krishna narrates the curious wonders they see along the way, including the groups of divine beings—Kinnaras, Siddhas, Vidyadharas, and others—who are enjoying the pleasures of the golden mountain. These divine beings are equally surprised to see humans like Krishna and Satyabhama in their area.[31] Krishna's accounts, akin to a travelogue, invoke a sense of *adbhuta,* wonder, in the idiom of Indian aesthetics. Once Krishna and Satyabhama arrive in the city of the gods, the women of the city rush to the windows and the terraces of the buildings, competing with each other for the right to catch a glimpse of Krishna as he passes by. This

genre of describing a king's procession before the women
of the city (known as *ulā* in Tamil poetry but found also
in many Sanskrit works) humanizes Krishna for his capti-
vating beauty.[32] It also humanizes the women of Indra's
city, who behave not like celestial Apsarasas but like human
women, teasing each other as they rush to watch Krishna
pass by in the royal path below.[33] Like any human women,
these women perspire and tingle at the thought of beholding
Krishna.

The narrative then shifts to the world of the gods, describ-
ing the wonders of Vaijayanta and the surrounding gardens,
which are resplendently decorated and attended by beauti-
ful women. Krishna and Satyabhama enjoy the pleasures of
Indra's garden, in which all of the seasons appear to converge
in one place.[34] After a day spent in luxury in Indra's heav-
enly realms, Krishna fearlessly enters the garden, uproots
the *pārijāta* tree, and secures it on Garuda's back. When the
gardeners begin to protest, Satyabhama is quick to respond:

"Listen, watchmen of Indra's garden!
Who is Shachi and who is Indra
to own this tree born from the ocean of milk?
Lakshmi and the precious gem Kaustubha
emerged with this tree,
and Vishnu took them.
If anyone should claim this tree
it is *he*.
This is not Indra's property.
Yes, I'm having my husband uproot it
and I'm taking it with me.

If your Shachi is really a hero's wife,
let her send her husband
to take it back from Krishna,
who obeys my every command."[35]

Does Satyabhama know that Vishnu, who had previously taken the Kaustubha gem and goddess Lakshmi from the milky ocean, and Krishna are one and the same god?

Timmana is ambiguous on this point. According to a traditional commentator, Vishnu, referred to in the verse simply as he, and Krishna are the same.[36] But if this reading is accepted, the second part of the verse conflicts with it, for there Satyabhama describes Krishna as *her* human husband. By contrast, the Sanskrit *Viṣṇu Purāṇa* is much clearer in this context, for there Satyabhama describes the *pārijāta* as "common to all the world."[37] For Timmana, the tree is the sole property of Vishnu and, by extension, Krishna: "If anyone should claim this tree it is *he*." The reading of this verse is further complicated by the fact that there is no indication in Timmana's entire poem that Satyabhama treats Krishna as anything other than a human husband; Satyabhama appears to have no knowledge that her husband is the god Vishnu himself.

When the gardeners hear Satyabhama's proud words, they relay everything to Indra, who, the poet takes care to note, is in the company of his wife Shachi. Indra, puffed with pride, belittles Krishna as a human cowherd.[38] Indra calls upon his lords of the directions, and together they wage war against Krishna. The battle that ensues between the god Indra and the human Krishna is filled with chaos and cacophony as the soldiers of Indra's army rush about trying to prepare for battle. Everyone is incredulous that Krishna, a mere human being, has taken the *pārijāta* tree. However, in the words of the poet, the battle drums resound as if they are crying out: "Don't go to battle with Krishna, the creator, protector, and destroyer of the universe. Don't be foolish!"[39]

Once the battle is underway and it becomes clear that Krishna's strength is unparalleled, the lords of the directions flee in fear. Indra, his anger intensified by this embarrassment, redoubles his efforts and, by himself, begins to attack Krishna, whom he still considers to be a mere human being. Indra mocks Krishna before shooting his diamond weapon, but Krishna catches the weapon easily in one hand, as if it were a lotus thrown at him in a game. Indra, stunned and speechless, falls at Krishna's feet and begs forgiveness. The sudden transformation in Indra enhances the impression of his cowardice and makes him look like a pretender to divinity.

Bidding farewell to Indra, Krishna and Satyabhama return to earth with the *pārijāta* tree by their side. As soon as the fragrance of the *pārijāta* spreads across Krishna's city Dvaraka, miracles begin to occur.[40] The people of Dvaraka become god-like when they smell the fragrance of the *pārijāta* flowers. While the human beings in Dvaraka acquire godliness, heavenly women themselves begin to wish they were human.[41] This envy of humans by the gods' women is a feature Timmana's text shares with Peddana's *The Story of Manu*. In Peddana's poem, the heroine, Varuthini, after failing in love with Pravara, envies human women who are lucky enough to die if their lovers reject them. As an Apsarasa, she has to live forever, suffering the pangs of love.

> Human women are lucky.
> If their lover rejects them, they die.
> But me—I'm immortal! I have to suffer
> this shameless sorrow. My beauty
> that cannot die is a lamp lit
> in an empty house.[42]

For the two major poets of this period, who produced the greatest poems of Telugu literature, the human being is the focus. For Peddana, who has a wider narrative canvas, the evolution of the human being is of primary importance. Peddana describes the birth of Svarochi, born from a godly mother and a Brahman father. As *The Story of Manu* progresses, we see the perfection of human qualities through the skills Svarochi acquires in medicine and languages. By the end of Peddana's text, a fully developed human being, Manu, is born. For Timmana, the canvas is somewhat smaller, but still tightly focused on the human world, in which god himself is viewed as fully human. Timmana envisions god as a human being and elaborately describes the glory of his human life, while never losing sight of Krishna's divinity.

Timmana's Sweet Words

In popular Telugu perception, Timmana's style is described with the phrase *muddupaluku* (sweet words), borrowed from an aphoristic verse from a different context.[43] A telling quality of Timmana's style is his effortless sweetness with words, which makes his verses flow gently. Worthy of special attention are his Sanskritic compounds, which are a hallmark of his poetic skill. For instance, let us examine the verse that describes Satyabhama crying before Krishna when she feels upset and neglected because of his preference for Rukmini.

> Burning with jealousy and grief,
> she pulled her sari over her face,
> delicate as a lotus in bloom,
> and wept softly before her husband,
> her voice sonorous like a cuckoo's
> raised on young mango shoots.[44]

Satyabhama's voice is described by the long compound—*bālapallavagrāsakaṣāyakaṇṭhakalakaṇṭhavadhūkalakākalīdhvanin*. It is a common literary convention to compare a woman's voice with that of a cuckoo's and to suggest that a cuckoo's voice sounds seductively sonorous when it chews on tender buds. The grace of Timmana's compound comes from his choice of words for buds (*bālapallava*), voice (*kaṣāyakaṇṭha*), and cuckoo (*kalakaṇṭha*), from among the many words available. The resulting alliteration of *ṭha* interspersed with a liquid *la* makes the compound flow like a gentle stream. The picturesque description of Satyabhama holding the end of her sari across her face while she cries makes the image even more striking. This verse is emblematic of Timmana's verbal craft and is noted by Telugu literati when comparing the three poets of this period: Peddana,

Timmana, and Bhattumurti, all of whom describe their heroines crying.

Timmana's vocative phrases, frequently used when addressing women, are equally appealing. For example, in the first chapter, Satyabhama is addressed with the following vocative:

O lalitendranīlaśakalopamakaiśika

Look, my dear with hair darker than blue sapphires.[45]

The image of Satyabhama's thick, dark hair integrated into the vocative addressed to her not only shows Krishna's admiration for her beauty, but also demonstrates the poet's skill in making words embrace one another. The ease with which Timmana makes his expressive compounds can also be seen in one of his final verses about his work: *ādivākaratārāsudhākaramuga* ("*to last as long as the sun, stars, and moon*").[46] Appearing like a matter-of-fact statement, this effortless cluster of words hides a telling suggestion about the lasting nature of Timmana's text by strategically using a long *ā* repeated through the compound, stretching it longer than its metrical limit.

Exemplary of Timmana's skill in crafting words is the following complex verse, which narrates an entire story in a single compound addressed to Krishnadevaraya:

Your hair stands on end with excitement
when you think of poems sung by good poets
who come every year for your spring festival.

You are even skilled at comforting your wives
when they suspect that you are excited
by thinking of another woman.[47]

Groups of good poets (*sukavinikara*) come together every year (*prativarṣa*) to attend, out of their own interest (*kutukāgata*), the spring festival (*vasantotsava*) conducted by Krishnadevaraya. They read their superb poems (*gumbhita-kāvya*). King Krishnadevaraya then remembers (*smṛti*) them at night and his hair stands on end (*romāñca*). The women of his inner chambers suspect (*viśaṅkita*) that the king is thinking of another woman. The king is an expert lover (*rasikā*) who is skilled at comforting them (*prasādana*). This entire narrative is seamlessly sewn together into an amazing single compound that ends in a vocative in praise of the king.

It is noteworthy that throughout the entirety of Timmana's poem, Satyabhama is described as a proud woman, enjoying the unrivaled attention of Krishna and commanding him to do her wishes. Only at the end of the narrative, when the *pārijāta* tree is planted in Satyabhama's garden, does Narada appear, once again for the purposes of advancing the human elements of the drama. Narada instructs Satyabhama to perform the *puṇyaka vrata,* a votive rite in which Satyabhama is required to give away the tree and her husband to a deserving Brahman. Narada tells Satyabhama to visit each of her co-wives' houses, free from anger, jealousy, and pride, and invite them to the rite.[48] Narada assures Satyabhama that if she completes this rite, she and her husband will live happily, their "hearts united as one, unattainable for anyone else."[49]

Satyabhama readily agrees to perform the rite and chooses

Narada himself as the deserving Brahman. However, when Satyabhama donates Krishna to Narada at the end of the *puṇyaka vrata,* she does so with full awareness that he will be returned to her. In her utterance of the mantra that is integral to the giving away (*dāna*), she says: *tubhyam ahaṁ sampradade namo namaḥ* ("To you I give. And I bow to you").[50] The chant that is usually uttered at the time of the ritual should be: *tubhyam ahaṃ sampradade na mama* ("To you I give. They are not mine anymore"). By saying *namo namaḥ* ("I bow to you") rather than *na mama* ("They are not mine anymore"), Satyabhama indicates that she does not relinquish her rights over her husband. Upon completion of the *puṇyaka vrata,* Narada gives Satyabhama back her husband and the *pārijāta* tree in exchange for all her ornaments.[51]

There is an important difference in tone between Timmana's text and the elaborate description of the *puṇyaka vrata* in Sanskrit sources, primarily the *Harivaṁśa* appendices.[52] The original intent of the *puṇyaka vrata* in these earlier sources is to teach Satyabhama to relinquish her control over her husband. In *Theft of a Tree,* however, there is no effort to discipline Satyabhama to become less possessive through the *puṇyaka vrata,* in the manner of the *Harivaṁśa,* or to elevate the devoted nature of Rukmini. In fact, Rukmini's presence in the *puṇyaka vrata* is described in rather unflattering terms.[53] Even in her departure, Rukmini is not given any special treatment, nor is she praised for her unrivaled devotion to Krishna. Instead, she is depicted as just one of the many wives who is sent off along with everyone else in the ritual.[54]

By the conclusion of Timmana's text, Satyabhama remains

as important as before, only prouder now that she has her wish fulfilled with the *pārijāta* tree in her backyard and her husband by her side. In effect, Timmana has changed the very nature of the *puṇyaka vrata* by making Satyabhama most important among her co-wives. Timmana relishes Satyabhama's human emotions. He portrays her as a woman who is angered by her husband, exercises her control over him, and then reconciles with him on *her* conditions. Krishna plays along as a human husband, with no indication that he is god. This focus on human emotions permeates the entirety of *Theft of a Tree,* which revels in the pleasures of human life.

On the Translation

We have chosen to translate most of the text into verse to reflect the range of meters used by the poet. However, there are several verses that are entirely prosaic in content, and we have translated them into prose (e.g., vv. 1.45–46). We have transliterated according to Telugu convention. Feminine nouns with long vowel endings in Sanskrit are all shortened in Telugu (e.g., *gopī* in Sanskrit is *gopi* in Telugu). We have marked the short *ĕ* and short *ŏ,* and the long *e* and *o* remain unmarked, as in Sanskrit. Proper names appear without diacritics and technical terms appear with diacritics and in italics.

Acknowledgments

We thank David Shulman, Archana Venkatesan, and Sheldon Pollock for carefully editing the English translation.

Thanks to Heather Hughes, Melissa Rodman, and Harvard University Press for their support. We thank Vadapalli Sesha Talpa Sayee for his meticulous and efficient typesetting and proofreading the Telugu text. We also thank our colleagues Joyce Burkhalter Flueckiger, Ilanit Loewy Shacham, and Kolavennu Malayavasini for their scholarly support and Paruchuri Sreenivas and Gautham Reddy for their bibliographic assistance. Finally, we are grateful to Naresh Keerthi for his support in identifying the botanical plants in the text.

NOTES

1   The *pārijāta* is a fragrant, flowering plant that can be called the Coral jasmine. In this text, the *pārijāta* is described as a heavenly tree that grants all wishes.
2   See Peddana 2015.
3   Chapter 5, v. 106.
4   Peddana 2015: 1.13–17.
5   Nannaya, *Mahābhāratamu* 1.16.
6   Whatever the veracity of this legend about Timmana, and it is very likely that the legend was created long after Timmana wrote *Theft of a Tree*, it demonstrates how the Telugu literary community views Timmana in relation to Krishnadevaraya and his wife Tirumaladevi. This legend also suggests that Timmana was closer to the queen than he was to the king, indirectly justifying why the poet does not describe the scene in which the king directly asked him to compose the poem.
7   Chapter 1, vv. 120–121.
8   Chapter 1, v. 17. See also ch. 1, v. 19.
9   Translation from Narayana Rao and Shulman 2002: 178.
10 See Narayana Rao and Shulman 1998: 135–200.
11 *Harivaṁśa Viṣṇuparva* 92.63–70. See also Austin (2013) for a discussion of the *pārijāta* episode in the critical edition and appendices of the *Harivaṁśa*.

12   See *Śrīviṣṇu Mahāpurāṇamu* 5.30.

13   Austin 2013: 250, n. 3. In the preface to Kavikarnapura's text, seven other Sanskrit *pārijāta*-centered texts are mentioned. See Kavikarnapura 2008: 12.

14   Austin 2013: 250.

15   See Tirupati Rao (2000) for a discussion of the Kannada text *Jagannāthavijaya;* Dehejia (2015) for a discussion of the *Sāralā Mahābhārata* from Orissa; and Smith (2007) for a discussion of the Maithili drama *Pārijātāharaṇa.*

16   Narayana Rao 2003: 302.

17   See the introduction to *The Sound of the Kiss or The Story that Must Never be Told* (Suranna 2002: xv–xxv).

18   Chapter 1, vv. 48–51.

19   Chapter 3, v. 38.

20   Chapter 3, v. 38.

21   For a more extensive discussion of *bandhakāvya,* see Timmanna 2022, pp. xxvi-xxix, and Kamath 2021.

22   Chapter 5, vv. 91–100. Also see ch. 5, v. 23.

23   Chapter 1, v. 60.

24   Chapter 1, v. 66.

25   Chapter 1, v. 82.

26   Chapter 1, v. 104.

27   Chapter 1, vv. 120–121.

28   Chapter 2, v. 19.

29   Chapter 2, v. 49.

30   Chapter 2, v. 53.

31   In ch. 2, v. 93, Krishna tells Satyabhama, "They are all surprised to see us here today."

32   See Peddana 2015: 587, n. 17.

33   Chapter 3, v. 12.

34   Chapter 3, v. 46.

35   Chapter 4, v. 58.

36   See commentary by Dusi (Timmana 1960: 284–285).

37   *Śrīviṣṇu Mahāpurāṇamu* 5.30.45–47, 51 is translated as follows:
       When they spoke like this, an angry Satyabhama said:
       "Who is Shachi and who is Shakra, the king of gods, to own
            the *pārijāta?*
       This tree, born at the time of the churning of the ocean,
       is common to all the world
       like the elixir of life, the moon, and Lakshmi.

The tree is like them, common to all the world...
I know that your husband is the lord of all gods
but still I, a human woman, am taking this *pārijāta* tree."

38 Chapter 4, v. 60.
39 Chapter 4, v. 63.
40 Chapter 5, vv. 46–47.
41 Chapter 4, v. 14.
42 Peddana 2015: 3.8.
43 The aphoristic verse mentioning Timmana's *muddupaluku* comes from Kakamani Murtakavi's *Pāñcālīpariṇayamu,* ch. 1.
44 Chapter 1, v. 133.
45 Chapter 1, v. 135.
46 Chapter 5, v. 106.
47 Chapter 1, v. 139.
48 Chapter 5, v. 57.
49 Chapter 5, v. 62.
50 Chapter 5, v. 82.
51 See ch. 5, v. 88.
52 See Austin 2013.
53 Chapter 5, v. 74.
54 Chapter 5, v. 90.

Theft of a Tree

Chapter 1

1

Shri, the auspicious goddess, [1]
plays on his chest,
adorned with the eternal Vaijayanti *
and the sparkling Kaustubha gem.
May that Venkateshvara
bless the son of Narasa,
King Krishnaraya.

2

When women lift up Parvati, the young bride,
to pour rice on Shiva's head, [2]
she sees her own reflection in the Ganga
and is sure there's another woman. She's jealous.
Shiva smiles. May he bless
Krishnaraya with vast power.

3

May the elephant god bestow
a mind as sharp as the tip of his tusk,
glory as high as his temples,
and energy equal to his youthful splendor.
With the gesture of his auspicious trunk,
may he bless Krishnaraya with long life.

---

* Vishnu's garland.

4

To end their lovers' quarrel,
Vishnu touches his bow, discus, sword, and conch
on Lakshmi's waist, hips, hair, and neck,[3]
and she's happy now.
May she always look kindly upon Krishnaraya,
the best of kings.

5

Sarasvati sings
gently plucking her vina's strings,
as if coaxing them
to follow the song in her voice.
May the light of her music
fill the heart of my king,
Krishnaraya.

6

He adorns the head of Shiva,
the son-in-law of the Snow Mountain,
he gives life to all the gods,
he is a source of endless coolness,
he is the vine that blossoms into light,
he is the son of the milky ocean.
May the moon shower Krishnaraya
with streams of compassion.

7

The moon gave birth to Budha, and Budha to Pururava. Pururava's son was Ayuvu. Ayuvu's son was Nahusha. Nahusha's son was Yayati. He, in turn, gave birth to the great warrior Turvasu.

8

In that great family of Turvasu, a king called Ishvara was born. He destroyed the pride of the strong arms of his bad enemies.

9

Ishvara, the god, is inactive. He's often violent. He's only half a man. He has a king, the moon, over his head. He lost to Arjuna, a mortal, in battle. The god Ishvara can't compare to our king Ishvara, dear to the earth.

10

They say that Parashurama killed every warrior and made their blood flow into a few pools. What's so great about that? Our king Ishvara fought a huge battle, conquering Bedanda fort. The blood that streamed from the Yavana soldiers filled thousands of rivers.[4]

11

To that perennial conqueror Ishvara and his wife Lakkambika, comparable to goddess Parvati herself, a son, Narasa, was born.[5] *Narasa's fame extended beyond the edges of the universe.*

12

The inscriptions declaring his conquests
    are as tall as the mountains at the ends of the earth.
The subordinate kings who pay him tribute
    are the rulers of the Kalinga and Yamuna lands.
The endless gifts he gives
    exceed his weight in gold.
The women of the heavens and land of snakes
    sing of his fame as an endless epic.
Seated on the towering throne of Vijayanagara, City of
    Victory, which mirrors the face of divine earth,
is the son of Ishvara,
the invincible King Narasa.

13

He conquered Bijapura
    and dragged King Kuntala by his hair. [6]
He ended the human life of the Parasika king
    when he conquered Manavadurga, the Human Fort. [7]
He sent the Chola king to kiss the sweet lips of the gods'
    women when he took the sweet city of Madhura. [8]
He showed the Yavana king of Srirangam
    how well his sword can dance.
Famous for giving sixteen kinds of gifts [9]
where Rama built his bridge,
he's known by the title "Sun in a Circle of Clouds."
He's the son of Ishvara,
the king, Narasa.

14

King Narasa, husband of the earth, had two wives from good families, Tippamba and Nagambika, equal to the wives of Vishnu, Earth and Wealth.

15

Tippamba had a son, Viranarasimha. He churned the ocean of his enemies like Mount Mandara and ruled the earth encircled by the sea.[10]

16

After Viranarasimha, Krishnaraya, the son of Nagamamba, ascended the throne, while his enemies ascended the hills, hiding themselves in thick forests. People were happy.

17

When he was Krishna
*   he couldn't sit on a throne because he was a cowherd.*
In those days he flirted with cowherd girls,
*   now he wants to be a brother to other women.*
He had to leave Mathura to his enemy Jarasandha,
*   now he wants to conquer every fort of every enemy.*
He stole the wish-giving tree from Indra,
*   now he gives instead of taking.*
He wants to improve the defects of his past life.
Krishna came back as Krishnaraya,
god himself in human form.

18

Redder than the pollen on the lotus from the navel of the god of
    Srirangam,
redder than the flowers adorning the breasts of Chola queens,
redder than the soil rich in ore that flows from the slopes of
    Sahya Mountain,
the waters of Kaveri flow red with the blood of his valiant
    enemy kings.

19

Krishna as Vishnu held the wheel,
    and Krishnaraya turns the wheel of dharma.
Krishna lifted the mountain and saved the cows,
    and Krishnaraya kills his enemy kings
    and saves the people.
Krishna was attached to his vaṃśa, *flute, in Brindavana,*
    and Krishnaraya is attached to his vaṃśa, *lineage,*
    and good people.
Krishna was in love with Satyabhama,
    and Krishnaraya loves satya, *truth,*
    and bhāma, *his wives.*
Krishna was born in a Yadava family,
and so is Krishnaraya.[11]
He is god Adinarayana* himself,
Krishnaraya, the son of Narasa.[12]

---

* Vishnu.

20

The earth goddess smiles at the pearls that adorn Krishnaraya's shoulders. Apparently, she remembers the unpleasant smell of the elephants' temples, which bore her burden, and the harsh touch of the stones on the hoods of the ancient snake.[13] *Now she enjoys the fragrant musk and brilliant ornaments on the shoulders of Krishnaraya, which carry her.*

21

Earlier, Shiva foolishly killed the love god Manmatha, Krishna's son. There's nothing noble about it. Krishnaraya protected Virabhadra, son of Prataparudra, showing compassion to the son of his enemy.[14]

22

Krishnaraya attacked the Utkala king and made his enemy's wife, the earth, fall in love with him. He knows the rite: when the broken trunks of the Utkala king's elephants were coiled like snakes making love, Krishnaraya covered them with the white cloth of his fame, enveloping the earth.[15]

23

He conquered Udayadri, the Morning Mountain,
    rising in power like the sun.
He took Vinukonda, the Listening Hill,
    simply by saying he'd do so.
He shook Kondavidu, the Hill Fort, and broke its peaks.
He smashed Bellamkonda, the Jaggery Hill,
    and crushed its blocks.

He ruined the pride of Devarakonda
  and struck the base of Jallipalli.
He pushed Anantagiri, the Hill of Snakes, under the earth.
He broke the steps of Kambambumettu,
  the City of Pillars and Steps.
The Utkala king is afraid his capital city Katakamu,
  the Anklet, will be stamped out.
The friend of all kings,
Krishnaraya is no ordinary king.

24

Krishnaraya's sword is like the long forehead mark of the
goddess Earth who plays on his shoulders. It's the oar that moves
the ship of victory through the ocean of his enemy armies. It's the
slate on which the goddess Conquest reads letters, written like
pearls, on the temples of enemy elephants. It's the magic wand
that unites his enemy kings with the women of the sky. If his
fame is the white half of Shiva, his sword is the other half, dark
like Parvati. It's the shadow, Chaya, that came in search of her
husband, the Sun. Krishnaraya's sword is many things in one.

25

For my king who has all these qualities—
for one who sends his enemies to heaven at the request of
  heavenly women and pleases Narada, who feeds on
  quarrels—

26

for one who gives more than any giver, outshining the
  legendary Karna—[16]
for one whose mind is always sharp—
for one who is kind to good scholars—

27

for the son of Nagambika—
for one whose fame surpasses all kings, past, present, and
  future, a fame that whitens the dark spots of the moon
  and the dark rut of the elephants that bear the earth—

28

for one who made the ocean delight in fresh rivers of blood
  flowing from the broken bodies of enemy armies,
  elephants, and horses—
for one who is an endless treasury in front of the houses of
  great scholars—

29

for one skilled as Drona in handling weapons—
for one who promotes the meaning of the Veda—
for one whose sword is still after a full meal of enemy flesh—

30

for one who makes the battleground frightening when his
  sword flicks its tongue like a snake that feeds on the
  breath of his enemies—

31

for one whose palaces swarm with bees blinded by the
fragrance of elephants from the Vindhya mountains and
whose glory poets describe in their books—
for one who knows the meaning of Manu's text—[17]

32

for one who is like the love god for all women—
for one who is praised by good people for giving more than the
sun, moon, and giving cow—

33

for one who is like fire scorching his enemies in battle—
for one who is refined in enjoying the arts—
for my hero, King Krishnaraya—

34

I write this epic poem, Theft of a Tree, *to bring him*
everlasting fortune. Listen to my story.

35

King Janamejaya listened to the beautiful stories of Vishnu
every day. Eager for more, he said to Vaishampayana:

36

"I am fulfilled listening to the stories of Hari. That enemy of
demons was born among the Yadus to help the gods. Why
did he bring to earth the *pārijāta* tree that sustains the gods?
Did they give it to him or did he take it by force? I want to

listen to you. Tell me every detail." Vaishampayana, Vyasa's
student, told him the following story.

37

After Krishna defeated Naraka,
he married, at Narada's suggestion,
sixteen thousand Apsarasas—
women eternally young,
imprisoned by that demon,
desiring only Krishna as their husband.

38

Before this, Krishna had eight wives,
Rukmini, Satya, Jambavati, Mitravinda,
Bhadra, Sudanta, Kalindi, and Lakshana,
all equally proud.

39

He spent time with all of them
in gardens on the outskirts of Dvaravati,
on man-made mountains,
in arbors near the seashore,
in pleasure palaces on riverbanks
paved with stones that melt in moonlight.

40

Any time, any woman, any game,
he was there.
Swimming in an ocean of happiness

in one of his thousand forms,
fully real in his illusion.

41

Though Krishna loved his wives equally,
he favored Rukmini, King Bhoja's daughter,
and Satyabhama, the daughter of King Satrajit.

42

Rukmini thought, "I am from a good family.
  I am beautiful. My husband loves me."
Satyabhama thought, "I am from a good family.
  I am beautiful. My husband loves me."
A great rivalry was born.

43

One day Krishna came to Rukmini's private palace. They sat
on a moonstone slab playing dice alone, served by women
with large eyes.[18]

44

Suddenly, from the sky, Narada appeared,
the sage who thrives on quarrels.
His vina, touched by the breeze,
      played the seven musical notes.
In his hand was a pot filled with
      water from the Ganga.
A string of prayer beads
      hung from his long ears.

His shoulders bore a satchel
    and a yak-tail fan for the dance of battle.[19]
His body glistened
like moonlight with no moon.
His matted locks looked like
leaf buds on the tree of liberation.[20]

45

Krishna, killer of demons, bowed before the sage. He and
his wife received the sage with deep devotion, as a guest of
honor.

46

Rukmini signaled with her eyes, and her servants brought
a jeweled throne for Narada. With the sage's permission,
Krishna sat beside him and respectfully said:

47

"Sage to the gods,
your arrival fulfills my desires.
You're always kind to me
for no particular reason."

48

The divine sage replied,
"Is it proper for you to speak
like a common man?
Don't I know your life story?
You're a blessing to all.

49

"You were the fish that entered the netherworlds and
   killed the thief of the First Words.*
You were the tortoise who bore the mountain on your back
   to help the gods get the elixir of life.
You were the boar that lifted the earth on the tips of your
   tusks.
You were the lion born from a great pillar at dusk to save
   your devotee.
You were the dwarf who stepped on the demon son of Diti.
You were the hero who destroyed all the kings of the earth.
You were the warrior who showered arrows across the
   ocean.
You are also you, now living in the city of Dvaraka.[21]

50

"You will ruin the honor of demons' wives.
You will end all sins of the present world.[22]
What more can I say?

51

"Because you're here,
Dvaraka is heaven,
and Rukmini is the goddess Lakshmi.
I long to visit you here again and again.
You are Kamsa's killer.
You are Mukunda, Murari."

---

* Vedas.

52

His heart full of joy, the sage gave Krishna a *pārijāta* flower
wrapped in a golden lotus leaf from the heavenly waters.
The flower buzzed with bees who seemed to be singing of its
fragrance, dripped with drops of honey as if it were shedding
tears of joy from being put to good use, and glistened with
the fame of fulfilling all desires.

53

Krishna took the flower,
astonished and grateful.
With Satyabhama on his mind,
he looked at Rukmini.

54

"If I give this to Rukmini,
who knows what Satya will say?
But if I send it to Satya with love,
Rukmini will be insulted.
Very well, since I'm here,
it's not proper to send it elsewhere."

55

With a nod from the sage,
Krishna gave the flower to Rukmini,
a smile on his face.
She took the flower,
bowed to the sage,
and tucked it in her hair.

Rukmini shone brilliantly
like the mountain king's daughter, Parvati,
crowned by Shiva's crescent moon.

56

Her shining eyes humbled the graceful fish,
her glistening breasts surpassed the round goose,
her black braid challenged the dark bees,
her radiant face outshone the red lotus.
By wearing that *pārijāta* flower,
her beauty was more beautiful,
her youth, more youthful,
her charm, more charming.

57

She was like a pearl,
newly polished.
Then Narada, eager for a fight,
grinned mischievously and said:

58

"Lotus-eyed lady, this is the *pārijāta* flower,
     impossible for humans to get.
Only the wives of the gods—
     Shachi, Parvati, Lakshmi, and Sarasvati—
     wear it every day.
It's clear that Krishna considers you
     his very life outside his body.
No one's equal to you
     among all these sixteen thousand women.

This flower is lucky to be worn by you.
If it's used properly,
it will give you anything you desire.
Let me tell you its powers.

59

"Its fragrance never spoils.
Its blossoms never fade.
Woman with a face like a lotus flower,
this king of flowers, filled with pollen,
is the only lovely thing in this world.

60

"When you are alone with your husband in secret play,
this flower acts like sparks from a flame,
enhancing joy in the game of love.
It also fans the sweat off your bodies
after you make love.
Use it as you wish.

61

"The moment you demand,
this flower prepares a delicious meal.
You'll never be hungry or tired.
It brings you fortune
that you cannot get in all three worlds.
Wear this flower
and surpass all other women
in pride and power.

62

"Wear this flower,
and other women will bow to your lotus feet.
Wear this flower,
and your husband will always love you,
never defying a single word.
Wear this flower,
and enjoy happiness, fortune, and fame.

63

"It brings coolness in summer and warmth in winter. It gives
you something new all the time.

64

"Among all women,
you excel in good luck.
Wear this this flower and,
as the saying goes,
no flower on your hair will ever wilt.

65

"All these days I hear that
Satyabhama commands Krishna with a single glance.
But I've never seen him show anyone else
the honor he gives you.
See, he has given this flower to you
and not her.

66

"Satya boasts that she is beautiful,
in the prime of her youth,
famous for her charms,
and her husband loves only her.
She dismisses all other women.
I'd love to see her face
when she hears what happened here.

67

"You can wear this flower for a whole year,
adorning your hair,
and then it goes back to where it came from,
the *pārijāta* tree in Indra's heaven."

68

The women in waiting who heard all this went back to their
queens and told them everything. The queens felt small.

69

Lakshana accepted the news,
thinking, "Rukmini is chief queen.
It's only fitting she get the flower."
Kalindi tolerated it.
Bhadra calmed down.
Sudanta let it go.
Jambavati didn't bother.
Mitravinda suppressed anger.

70

At the time, Satya, the most beautiful and proud among
them, was thinking to herself: "My friend who went to visit
Krishna hasn't returned since morning."

71

In her palace gardens
on a moonstone slab dusted with pollen,
beside a stream flowing from a river of nectar,
the queen sat with her friends
chatting about Krishna's many virtues.

72

"The buzzing of bees,
the sweet songs of cuckoos rustling through thick leaves,
the cool breeze from lotus ponds—
they're no longer pleasing as before.
Something's not right," she said to her friend.

73

"I don't know what it is but
my right shoulder, nipple, and eye
are quivering,
and that's not good.[23]
There's a certain sadness in my mind.
I'm scared.
Maybe my dear husband has found
some other young woman
and is doing something I won't like."

74

While Satyabhama was talking to her friends, a friend
suddenly ran up, her eyes red as the setting sun, and said:

75

"Dear lady! I don't know how to tell you. When your husband
was with Rukmini, the sage Narada appeared.

76

"He gave Krishna a special flower,
praising it as flawless,
only fit for the gods,
saying it gives great happiness,
and no one else can get it.

77

"Bursting with joy, Krishna
took the flower and pressed it to his eyes.
He bowed to the sage and gave the flower
to Rukmini, and she tucked it in her hair.

78

"She looked splendid,
glistening with a new glow that can't be described,
like the love god's arrow, newly sharpened.

79

"With the power the flower has given her,
Rukmini, that woman with shining eyes,
looked like she was sitting on a high pedestal of glory,
ruling the three worlds,
as all the other women served her,
without a trace of jealousy in their minds.

80

"But Narada didn't stop there.
With Krishna listening,
and Rukmini listening,
and me listening, he said,
'That woman Satya thinks
there is no one equal to her
and she is the one Krishna loves best.
This will be the end of her pride.'

81

"Anyone who saw the games
of Narada, the sage who thrives on quarrels,
and the airs of Rukmini,
and Krishna's doings,
would be angry.
Anyone."

82

Hearing these words, Satyabhama rose
like a wounded snake ready to strike,
like a flaming fire fed with ghee.
Her eyes blazed, red as
the saffron designs freshly painted on her cheeks.
Her voice choked with anger,
she spoke:

83

"Say it again?
That meddlesome sage who lives on quarrels
arrived and said all this?
Did that lover of cowherd girls
listen to all these things with his own ears?
And what did Rukmini say?
Don't hide anything from me.
Tell me everything.

84

"I don't care if Narada made a big thing of that flower
and gifted it to Krishna to get on his good side.
I don't even care if Krishna gave it to whoever he likes.
But why should he bring me into it,
that liar of a sage?

85

"It may be natural for a sage who wanders the world
to tie people into knots with words,
as if quarrels bring him good luck.
But shouldn't my husband stop him from speaking?

86

"All right, the sage gave the flower, and Rukmini took it.
We can't blame them for what they did.
But that tricky cowherd, he's to blame.
If your husband acted like this,
your heart would surely burn.

87

"Men don't look at their own actions,
but say that women's love can't be trusted.
It's men who can't be trusted.
Their minds are fickle
like wisps of autumn clouds.

88

"All these days my beloved watched over me
like an eyelid protecting the eye.
I was the best among all these women.
Now my co-wives turn up their noses at me
and gossip behind my back.
I still cling to life, but I don't know why.

89

"He should be admired for his skill.
He kept me happy all these days
while playing games
hiding his love for Rukmini.
I should praise him,
that master of deception.

90

"The sage brought a flower,
gifted it to Krishna,
he gave it to that woman.
I've suffered all this
and I'm still alive.
I wonder what else is in store.

91

"The world knows who helped him and who didn't.[24]
That killer of Naraka, he knows.
And Rukmini too.

92

"Krishna happened to be in that woman's house,
so he gave her a flower because it made sense.
But why should all the other wives fall at her feet,
abandoning their honor, dignity, propriety,
glory, self-respect, wisdom?
I am surprised.

93

"My friend,
to have a man
who moves through his wife's mind
like a string through a pearl
is surely the fruit of past good deeds.

94

"Even in dreams, even in jest,
      he was afraid to cross my word.
He never gave anyone anything
      without giving it to me first.
He bribed my girlfriends to make sure
      they wouldn't tell on him.
He became impatient when
      my co-wives asked for equal treatment.
We were totally in love,
our desires endless.
We were always one, inseparable.
How could such a man do this today?

95

"We used to play hide-and-seek in mountain caves,
celebrate the marriage of the vine and tree,
tug at each other's clothes after winning at dice,
worry when the lovebirds were torn apart at nightfall,[25]
run playfully in the moonlight,
rest on cool milk-white moonstones,
meditate on each other's portraits drawn on wooden slabs.

Has he forgotten all of this,
lost in Rukmini's maya?

96

"A husband is life itself.
A husband is god.
He protects you in seven ways.[26]
If he crosses the line,
does a woman have any recourse?

97

"If a husband gives money and takes it back,
a wife can accept it.
But if a husband gives love and takes it back,
can a wife survive?"

98

Suffering an endless grief,
her anger rising,
that slender woman went to her anger chamber,[27]
like a female snake that moves
into her hole in a sandalwood tree.

99

She put on a soiled sari,
cast off her ornaments,
tied a cloth around her head,
smeared musk on her forehead,
all with a heavy heart.

Tormented by the god of love,
she tossed and turned on her bed in a dark room,
like the crescent moon at the edge of a black cloud.

100

She fainted, overcome with grief.
She shuddered, began to sweat.
Her heart grew heavy, filled with sadness,
the poison of envy grew inside.
Love was like snakebite now, only worse.

101

She closed her eyes slowly
and opened them.
She laughed, shook her head,
fell on the bed, sighed.
She rose, she stumbled.
She was frantic.
Jealousy and anger grew inside her.
Tormented with desire,
her charm and beauty destroyed,
she was like a lotus
trampled by an elephant.

102

Satyabhama gave herself over to anger and sadness.
Burdened by grief, she stopped everything else. Meanwhile,
Krishna thought:

103

"Satya's friend saw it all.
She watched me offer the flower
to Rukmini that Narada gave me.
She's surely spinning some stories about me."
His mind filled with worry, Krishna
entrusted the sage to his son Pradyumna

104

and mounted his chariot.
His patience shaking like the edges
of the flag fluttering above him,
he drove the horses faster.
His mind spinning
like the wheels of his chariot,
he went forth, in a panic,
along the path to Satya's palace.

105

He dismounted and ordered his charioteer to wait outside.
He crossed the courtyards on foot, finding the palace
strangely silent.

106

"Where are the women in waiting who make the parrots
    sing by feeding them sugar?
No one is making the peacocks dance, keeping the beat
    with their clapping hands.
No one is playing the vina, flicking the strings with their
    fingernails.

Nobody gathers the baby geese, teaching them to walk.
The palace is not like every day.
Its beauty gone, the palace looks small.
Someone must have told Satya the story of the flower."

107
Krishna moved quietly to the anger room
where Satya lay, a veil covering her.
He softly stepped in,
true to his tricks.

108
With gentle whispers, sharp glances, a flick of his wrist,
he coaxed Satya's maids to his side.
He approached her, wilted like a tender leaf
scorched by the midday sun.

109
"Let's see what's going on,"
thought the wily cowherd.
Standing behind her,
he picked up a fan from Satya's maid
and began to fan her,
as if stirring the flames of her desire.

110
Suddenly, traces of fragrance from the divine flower spread.
Surprised by the new smell, Satyabhama removed her veil,
looked around the room, and saw her husband holding the
fan. Her eyes filled with tears.

111

She pulled the veil back
and lowered her head.
Tears streamed down her soft cheeks
like drops of honey on a leaf.

112

Krishna, body dark as a raincloud,
came to cool this woman's mind.
The edges of the veil rose
with her warm breaths,
as if a breeze, the friend of fire,
had come to rekindle her desire.

113

The saffron designs painted on her breasts
melted in the endless beads of sweat
and seeped into the edges of her white silk sari,
as if she were straining the essence of anger
pouring from her heart.

114

That proud woman,
overtaken by endless anger and pride,
sat there in grief.
Krishna, his mind full of love, said:

115

"My dear, you're not wearing any jewels.
You never give up those soft red saris.
Why are you wearing simple white today?
Your tender lips are missing the gloss of red betel.
You don't look like yourself.
Tell me what's wrong.

116

"Is this a game to test my love?
Is this a joke? Do you want to scare me?
Tell me, have I done something wrong?
Am I your enemy?
Why do you look at me like this?
I can't live another moment without your love.

117

"You're not speaking words sweet as honey.
You don't look at me with shy glances.
You don't hold me tight,
pressing your breasts against my chest.
Why this distance between us?
My pet parrot, has anyone done something to you?
Why are you upset?

118

"In thought, word, or deed,
I don't love any other woman.
I give them respect, just for show.

My real passion is for you alone.
I'm like a king when I act on your command.

119

"If I don't deserve a kiss from your sweet lips
or an embrace in your arms,
at least give me a glance from your wide eyes."
He couldn't resist,
pulling the end of her sari from her shoulder.
She threatened him,
trying to hit him with the lotus in her hand.

120

He saw no way to appease the anger in her heart.
Nothing was working.
Krishna, master puppeteer who pulls the strings of the
      world,
bowed down to her feet, soft as the lotus,
their redness heightening the radiance of his jeweled
      crown.

121

She kicked him with her left foot,
right on the head—
a head worthy of worship by Brahma and Indra,
the head of the father of the love god.
That's how it is.
When a husband crosses the line,
does an angry wife know what she's doing?

122

At that angry kick, Krishna felt a thrill.
The fake cowherd spoke in a passion,
showing all his love.

123

"Your kick is an honor to me,
your humble servant.
But your tender feet must have been pricked
by the bristling hairs on my body.
Please don't be angry, my dear."

124

She stood up,
her sari slipping from her shoulder,
revealing half her body.
She fixed her loose hair again and again,
tucking it back into its bun,
and covered her breasts with the edge of her sari.
There were beads of sweat on her face,
and her eyes shot threatening looks.
She spoke, lips trembling.

125

"Stop this pretense, this false love, these nice words.
I trusted you and look what happened.
You loved me and now you've tossed me aside.
You don't know how people are laughing at me.
What would a cowherd know about love?

126

"I don't trust you anymore.
Why are you trying to excite me?
I can see through your lies, they're not to my taste.
Maybe Rukmini will like them.
Lover of gopis, enough is enough.
Don't tease me anymore with love you don't have.

127

"Tricks and lies were born with you,
fed to you as a child along with milk and butter.
I knew that, but still, I trusted you.
I've lost my honor and pride. What can I do?

128

"The sage gave you the flower
and praised that woman, your dear wife.
Your ears heard sweet words of praise,
and now you have to listen to my boring talk.
You come here reeking of that flower
just to mock me.

129

"Pride is a woman's jewel.
Pride is greater than life.
Pride is the source of all respect.
Without pride in herself,
can a woman live?

130

"Among all her daughters-in-law,
your mother Devaki
treated me as the best,
because you loved me.
I'll be ashamed to see her now.

131

"I wonder which lucky woman will wear the Syamantaka
    jewel on her hair.
Which one will play by the dovecotes on the slopes of
    Raivataka Mountain?
Who gets the house in the spring garden surrounded by
    fragrant banana plants?
Who'll watch the waves with you through the lattice
    windows of this jeweled palace?
The parrots, peacocks, and mynahs that I raised—
    I guess they'll go to some other woman.
Don't worry, I promise to make you happy
even before they all start laughing.

132

"Who do you think I am?"
Her eyes welled up, she bent her head low
and, her voice choked with tears,
she could speak no more.

133

Burning with jealousy and grief,
she pulled her sari over her face,

delicate as a lotus in bloom,
and wept softly before her husband,
her voice sonorous like a cuckoo's
raised on young mango shoots.

134

Unable to contain the anger in her heart, she wept. Krishna embraced her, consoling her with sweet words, wiping the tears streaming down her cheeks. He said in a gentle, friendly voice:

135

"Look, my dear with hair darker than blue sapphires,
why are you grieving for just one flower when I'm right
     here?
Listen, I'll bring you the whole tree.
I'll go to Indra's garden and get the *pārijāta,*
even if he, the king of the gods, wages war.

136

"I'll plant it in your garden,
next to the pond of red water lilies that spreads coolness
and among the fragrant banana trees—
right here in your backyard.
Watch it grow and be happy."

137

He spoke those words in his voice, deep as a rain cloud. Satya brightened up like a *nīpa* tree surrounded by peacocks, her friends.[28]

138

Krishnadevaraya,
your eyes are full of compassion,
you strive for the good of the world,
you send your enemy kings to heaven
to embrace the breasts of Rambha, the divine woman,
your fame spreads in all directions,
you are a peaceful man at heart,
your policies follow the texts,
you plan strategically, informed by spies,
you are praised by poets.

139

Your hair stands on end with excitement
when you think of poems sung by good poets
who come every year for your spring festival.
You are even skilled at comforting your wives
when they suspect that you are excited
by thinking of another woman.

140

You are the love god to all women,
you illuminate the faces of the women of the directions
with the white sandal of your fame
mingled with a touch of vermillion,[29]
your good name is wide as your arms,
your sword is smeared with the blood of enemy kings,
you are the best of the lunar family.

CHAPTER 1

Timmaya of the Kaushika lineage,
Singaya's son, blessed by Shiva with poetic skill,
composed this great poem, Theft of a Tree.
This is its first chapter.

Chapter 2

1

King Krishnaraya,
you live in Malayakuta palace where
supplicants swarm like bees to
drink the steady stream of mercy from your eyes,
wide as the lotuses where Lakshmi lives.

2

Vaishampayana to Janamejaya:

After he vowed to steal the *pārijāta* tree, Krishna went to the Moon Pavilion.

3

With sweet words and amusing stories, he set Satya afloat on an ocean of love. They were lost in play when they heard the call of the conch announcing the noon hour.

4

Knowing Krishna's routine, Satyabhama glanced at her attendants, and they stepped forward and stood obediently.

5

One woman,
slender as a tender leaf,
announced the bath,
calling Krishna
with musical words and a gentle laugh,
sweet as a vina's melody.

6

Joyfully, Krishna looked at Satya, queen of his heart,
eyes smiling, he said: "Let's go bathe."
He took the hand of a woman with bright eyes,
descending the throne,
the edge of his golden upper cloth slipping slightly.
The guards of the inner palace cried, "*Samukhā!*"
calling everyone to attention.

7

One woman slipped
golden sandals on his feet,
red as if touched by vermillion
adorning the hair of women,
the First Words.[1]

8

Moving gracefully, he went to the bathing hall. Resting on
a seat studded with sapphires, Krishna carefully removed
Kaustubha and his other gems, one by one.

9

One woman, her face bright as the moon,
massaged Krishna's head with *campaka* oil,
her thin waist swaying, her breasts dancing,
forehead sweating, necklaces jingling, bangles tinkling.

10

Another shook out his hair,
dark as black bees escaping her lotus hands,
squeezing it dry, combing it with her fingernails
scenting it with perfumed water and *āmla* essence.[2]

11

As women passed golden pots,
one of them bent down
and poured water on the Yadava king,
her arms shining,
hair loose across her breasts.

12

A woman with a delicate body dried him with a soft cloth,
    yellow tinged with reddish hues.
Another with a delicate figure combed his long hair with
    her fingernails, gently untangling it.
A woman, her face round as the moon,
    handed him clean clothes white as moonlight.
A woman with a voice sweet as a parrot's
    adorned him in nine kinds of gems.
Another, her body fragrant as a lotus,
    handed him flower garlands.

One, her eyes glowing, rubbed sandal paste on his body.
A woman fanned him with a whisk scented with camphor,
and another placed a standing mirror before him.

13

Some women waved pearl lamps
in a new way:
the gleam of their wide eyes
and the jeweled lamps of the palaces
trading places.

14

To her husband's delight,
trailed by a line of royal geese
following the sound of her gold anklets,
Satyabhama arrived with her friends—
freshly bathed, dressed in fine clothes,
decked in jewels, fragrant with rare perfumes,
a crimson lotus tucked into her bun.

15

Like a full moon peeking through clouds of envy,
a fragrant lotus blooming after an endless night,
a quiet pond resting after an elephant plunged in,
a jasmine vine flowering after scorching summer,
her heart blossomed, free from grief.
His beloved Satya stood before Krishna.
Just then,

16

Narada, the sage who lives on quarrels, arrived, after taking leave of Rukmini and finishing his midday rites near the ocean.

17

Satya and Krishna received him as a guest of honor, as befitting the occasion. Two women came and announced that food was served. Satya and Krishna followed the sage to the dining hall as a streak of lightning and a dark cloud follow the moon.

18

Krishna sat down for the meal next to the sage. Along with him sat Samba and his other sons, Satyaki and his other brothers, and all their relatives. Women with eyes wide as lotuses gently fanned them, spreading a cool breeze.

19

Young women, tender as spring flowers, served the meal.
Their bracelets clinked,
      praising the delicious food.
Their girdles studded with gems tinkled,
      as if saying, "Hurry up! Serve them now!"
The folds of their white saris rustled,
      whiter than the white rice.
Their toe rings tapped on the floor,
      calling the guests to eat more and more.

Narada and Krishna ate with joy,
praising the tastes of all five kinds of food—
eaten, chewed, relished, sucked, and drunk.[3]

20

Along with his relatives,
Krishna washed his hands
in perfumed water poured
from the edges of golden vessels tipped
by the hands of bright-eyed women.

21

Krishna ordered the attendants to give betel and camphor
to all his guests. Meanwhile, his wife

22

finished her meal in the inner palace.[4] She came to Krishna
in the Moon Pavilion and bowed to Narada's feet.

23

The sage spoke:

24

"You and your husband are inseparable.
People honor you.
Relatives praise you.
Your co-wives envy you.
You have glory, power, and position.
What blessings can I give you,
as if you were an ordinary woman?

25

"Your husband goes nowhere without you,
not even to battle.
He loves you as his own life,
gives everything you ask.
You are closer to him than anyone.
You are lucky.
I have not heard of a woman like you
anywhere in the world.

26

"But still I bless you. May your husband do your bidding,
leaving everything else undone. This is my blessing."

27

The sage turned to Krishna, "I will take leave of you. Do not
forget me." Krishna, the god who plays games with girls who
watch the cows, suddenly had an idea.

28

"Naraka tricked Aditi, the mother of gods, and stole her
earrings. I killed that demon, retrieved the earrings and
have kept them carefully ever since. Indra hasn't sent for
them. Am I a stranger? Tell the king of gods that I will bring
them myself."

29

Krishna bade farewell to Narada,
the sage who lives on quarrels.
The lord of the world
played dice with Satyabhama
until the sun touched the peaks
of the Western Mountain,
glowing redder than the
wide eyes of gopis
drunk on liquor.

30

Darkness, lurking in silence, watched the defeated Sun depart to Sunset Mountain. He quickly ordered his soldier Dusk to grab the Sun's wife, Shadow. The evening calls of the birds—*Ko! Ko!*—sounded like her cries of protest as Dusk dragged her away.[5]

31

Lovebirds turned away from the setting sun, only to see its reflection in the lotus pond below. As they fainted from grief, lotuses began to close, as if the goddess Water had shut her eyes, crying out at the sad scene. Can you bear a friend's torment?

32

The elephant Sky, filled with darkness, grew wild with pride.
He hurled the Sun, who was riding him, onto the slopes of
Sunset Mountain, shattering his body, and the Sun threw up
blood. That's the red you see in the western sky.

33

A bee, crazy for another, left his wife, drunk on honey, in
their lotus home. He returned in the evening and found
himself locked out when the petals closed. Like the night
watchman, he wandered aimlessly, a thankless job.

34

As Darkness spread across the earth,
some thought Day was the ocean,
    and Night the dregs left by Agastya
    after he gulped it down.[6]
Others imagined the fire of dusk burning the forests,
    and the smoke of night rising from Sunset Mountain.
For some, the dark sky lost the sun, its precious jewel,
    and descended to earth in search of it.
For others, ink was rubbed onto the sky,
    and the stars were letters
    inscribing the love god's victory.
Some thought Darkness the hair dye
aging courtesans use to look young again,
or was it the liniment that makes adulteresses invisible
so they can move freely in secret?

35

Young women, eager for secret trysts, prayed:
"Love God, we'll give you
    a parrot chariot, sugarcane bow,
    and dark lotus arrows.
Lord Krishna, we'll give you
    a flower garland, new flute, and peacock feathers.
Goddess Kali, you're dark yourself, we'll give you
    a black shawl, some musk, and fresh kohl.
Ganesha, god with an elephant's face, we'll give you
    a rose apple, a dark fan, and stalks of grass.
Darkness works for the welfare of the world.
Free him from the evils of sun and moon.
We beg you:
make him last forever."

36

Rows of lamps began to flicker
from the deep sighs of women
kept from their lovers by domestic chores.
New rings of smoke circled those lamps
with the promise of fresh kohl,
as if to say, "Don't worry, we'll protect you."

37

The stars appeared in the sky.
Are they hail rained down by dense clouds of darkness?
Could they be crystal bullets shot by the moon
    through the barrel of his beams to separate lovebirds?

They look like piles of moonlight heaped up by the gods'
    girls on the sandy shores of the heavenly river.
Or are they the holes of a silversmith's plate
    through which moonbeams are pulled?
Perhaps they're grains of white rice sprinkled on
    Manmatha*
by his wife, blessing him as he sets out to conquer the
    world.
Maybe they're beads of sweat on the body of the sky,
scorched by the sun.

38

The eastern sky turned white
even before the moon appeared.
Could this be the face of Fortune, Indra's royal queen,
that grew pale when she saw
Krishna going to steal the *pārijāta*
for his beloved wife Satya?

39

Slowly, the rays of the moon crept across the eastern sky.
They could be tusks of the elephant Time
    rushing to cut down the tree of Darkness,
maybe they are the tender first leaves of the screw pine
    growing on the edges of the eastern sky,
or are they streaks of sandal paste plastered
    on the walls of the labor room, the Eastern Mountain?

----

* The love god.

Perhaps they're silver canes in the hands of watchmen
    clearing a path for the love god
or crystal canals guiding moonlight to water lilies?
Slowly, very slowly,
streaks of light slipped across the sky.

40

The Moon climbed the sky,
full in his shining body,
as if the gods were pulling on
the silver ropes of a crystal bucket
filled with the elixir of life
from the ocean of immortality.

41

The gods see him as a horn of plenty. The Sun respects him as
a companion. He's a killer of darkness. He makes the water
lily smile. He's bad luck for adulteresses. New lotuses shy
away from him out of respect. He breaks the hearts of love-
birds. The Moon, scattering light, rose in the eastern sky.

42

Imagine that Dusk is a farmer who planted the sun, a banana
tree, on the shores of the western ocean. The dark evening
clouds are its leaves, and its fruit in the east is the glowing
moon.[7]

43

Time, the practiced lover, was stringing a necklace of rubies
and pearls, one by one, on a string that is dusk. By mistake,

he added a ruby, the sun, out of place. Then he threw it off and put a pearl there instead. The pearl was the moon, and its hole was the dark spot you see on the moon.

44

The Woman of the West, eager to adorn the goddess Evening, dropped her cotton headband, which had a red lacquer dot, the sun, into the middle of the ocean. After squeezing out the red hues of dusk, she threw away the cotton. That's why the moon looks colorless and pale.

45

Night, who is the love god, intent on uniting Shiva with Parvati, shot arrows of stars at him. An angry Shiva burned that darkness with his fiery third eye and smeared the ashes on his body. Now Shiva is the ash-white moon.

46

The dark spot on the moon was like a setting missing its gem, dislodged as the Woman of the East scraped against the jagged slopes of the Eastern Mountain. Or maybe it was black kohl lining the eyes of the woman, Night.

47

The scene of moonrise seems like the story of Balarama and the river Yamuna reenacted. Moonlight, like liquor, intoxicates Balarama. The redness of its rising is like his body lotion. The dark spot is the black clothes he wears. Darkness ran in fear like black Yamuna. The rays of the moon are his plow, drawing a line to force the river to flow toward him.

The light of the full moon is the river Ganga as she came to comfort the frightened Yamuna.[8]

48
A fine mist spread, as if the Moon were sweating from pleasure as he held the hands of his young bride, the Water Lily.

49
Female *cakora* birds served a feast of moonlight
in celebration of the love god.
They added new moon rays to hot moonlight
    fresh from the bodies of separated lovers
    and made it warm and delicious.
From moonlight fallen from the pollen of water lilies,
    they strained the bitter taste with
    a fine mesh of moon rays.
Into liquid moonlight dripping from moonstones
    they mixed thick moon rays, making its texture
    creamy and smooth.
To the perfumed moonlight from women's bodies
    they added gentle moon rays, making a fragrant drink.
Male and female birds sitting in a row,
ate happily, joking among themselves.

50
Dark clouds that are women's pride scattered. White lilies glowed brightly like *rĕllu* reeds.[9] Darkness melted away like mud. Moonlight shone clear. The redness of the evening sky faded. White lotuses and jasmine flowers closed. The ocean

of desire of young lovers reached high tide. Geese became agitated, as lovebirds do. Flashes of lightning hid themselves like women unable to meet their lovers for secret trysts. During that autumn night, the love god strung his bow and waged war on separated lovers.

51

The bells of the clock in Krishna's palace chimed like the twang from the bow of the love god, tormentor of women unable to meet their lovers in secret. Women angry with their husbands heard the bells toll at the end of the first watch and rushed back to make love before night's end.[10]

52

"Dress all in white,
wear pearls around your neck,
put sandal paste on your body,
and tuck jasmine in your hair.
Nobody will see you,
even if you brush past them,"
said their girlfriends,
urging women to go in search of their lovers
in the flooding moonlight.

53

The shining rays of moonlight were like:

reflections of Shiva's wild laughter as he dances in fury at
the end of the day;

replacements for rows of sand scattered by the tip of the
trunk of Indra's elephant Airavana playing on the
sandy banks of the eastern ocean;[11]

replications of streams of water from the heavenly Ganga
spouting from the toe of time when he stepped on
darkness, just like Vishnu stepped on the demon-king
Bali.

The moon's rays:

flowed from palaces built with moonstones like water falling
from the peaks of the Himalayas, rushing downward to break
the riverbanks, which are the defenses of proud women;

filled the open caves that are the beaks of lovebirds, crying
from the pain of unbearable separation;

twirled around blooming red water lilies;

rolled on piles of pollen falling from flowers shaking in the
gentle breeze, becoming whiter;

touched the shining cheeks of proud women rocking joyfully
on golden swings;

cleared away darkness thick as a forest of black trees;

immersed the world in whiteness;

covered Brahma's egg, the universe, in a silver coating.

There were moonstone vessels melting in moonlight, eager to be filled, and containers laced with delicious camphor. Filling them with wine, a pair of lovers drank to their delight, tasting each other's lips as an appetizing relish. Getting drunk, they reveled under a flowery lattice.

A young couple relaxed on beds of pollen beneath bowers after applying a mixture of camphor, musk, civet, and sandalwood cream on each other, as if protecting their bodies from losing luster after making love.

Experienced girlfriends pushed a newly married couple, filled with shyness toward each other, and left. The love god himself hastened the battle of love-play, calling forth his soldiers to shower sharp arrows on them. Their defenses gone, they stole glances at each other, thinking the other was not looking at them, and finally gave themselves to making love in a hidden spot.

When a young couple met, they embraced each other's excited bodies tightly as if making their hearts melt into one. They spoke of how much they missed each other during the day and became entwined on a bed of down, lost in limitless joy.
A couple began to miss each other after a lovers' quarrel. The fire of separation flared up under the heat of the full moon. When it became unbearable, they tricked their friends and crept off to a secret spot to make love.

A young woman, proud of her breasts taut with desire, and a young man, contesting her pride, tried to outshine one another. They made love in various postures and actions, supported by the love god's thirty-two arrows.[12]

A youthful couple, lost in desire, rested on moonstone slabs, savoring the secrets of the science of love and forgetting everything outside them, like sages deep in meditation.

A young couple, exhausted with endless games of love, limbs trembling, rested on each other and gently rocked on a swing, their eyes half-closed.

With all these couples, the city of Dvaraka resembled the kingdom of the love god.

In that city,
in a palace illumined by brilliant gems serving as lamps,
decorated with pure white drapes,
shining with alcoves brightened by hanging bunches of
    pearls,
sparkling with crystal walls adorned with colorful
    paintings,
splendid with a jeweled cot covered with a quilt of soft
    goose feathers,
brilliant with emerald plates filled with areca nuts and
    tender betel leaves,
adorned with oyster cups filled with sandal paste mixed
    with musk,
beautiful with fans made of newly blossoming flowers,

delightful with flower garlands strung with the tender
    fibers of lotus stalks,
perfumed with fragrant black incense,
resplendent with golden pitchers filled with cool scented
    water,
pleasant with cooing sounds of doves and other birds,
and shining with mirrors laden with fine gems,
Krishna and Satya made love and rested, their eyes heavy
    with sleep.
At that time,

54

Shukra, the morning star, the jewel on the hood of serpent
Time, was afraid that the stars, his relatives, would be
destroyed by the rising sun. Shukra appeared first in the
sky to encourage his disciples, the dark Mandeha demons,
to battle the Sun.[13]

55

Singers composed songs
sweet as honey
to awaken Yashoda's son
with enchanting morning melodies.

56

"You are Govinda, Mukunda,
you bear the discus,
you destroyed Kamsa,
Satyabhama loves you,
you are Narayana,

61

you are adorned with the gem Kaustubha,
you protected Gajendra,
you destroyed Kaliya's pride,
you ride on Garuda,
you wear the eternal Vaijayanti,
you are called Krishna, Vaikuntha, Shauri,
you are Yashoda's son,
you are kind to your devotees, Murari,
gopis love you.

57

"You reside amid the ocean,
wielder of Sharnga,
good people meditate on you,
the sun and moon are your eyes,
a white lotus in your navel,
jewel among warriors,
you sleep on Shesha,
the Primordial Snake,
lifter of Govardhana,
effulgent one, heroic bearer
of the disc and conch,
Shiva worships you.[14]

58

"Wake up, Krishna!
Parrots are babbling sweet syllables and,
hungry for more,
wake women, their teachers,
eyes heavy with sleep.

59

"The moon looks like a piece of dung
    from the heavenly cow
    burned to ashes by wild fires of the western sky.
Or is it a beehive sucked empty by bees
    like the moonlight savored by *cakora* birds?
Or is it a bun of white hair on the old woman Night
    slowly moving toward the west?
Perhaps it's the ball of cloth rolled up by artist Time
    after painting palaces in the sky.[15]
No, it must be a cluster of flowers,
on the vine of moonlight.
The moon has lost its light,
a shadow of itself,
it sets in the western sky.

Won't you wake up,
lord with lotus eyes?

60

"At day's end, the Sun, afraid that the dark night might steal
his splendor, entrusted his light to the night lamps of the
house, and they shone brightly all night.

In the early morning, the Moon, lord of the stars, fearful of
the day's heat, gave away his light to the same lamps, and
now they glow pale as the moon.

61

"Sleepy-eyed elephants
stand guard by the hour at the palace gates,
their cheeks buzzing with bees,
their ears keeping rhythm with the morning singers,
their trunks swaying in time.

62

"Krishna, the young cowherd who is Time,
killed the demon Putana, the night,
sucking dry streams of milky light
from her moon-shaped breasts
mixed with poison, the dark spot on the moon.
Her starry eyes drooped,
and her breath became thick as the wind at dawn.[16]

63

"Krishna,
look at those tender leaf buds damp with dew
like lips, red as *bimba* fruit,
wet with tears shed by women,
sad, separated from you.[17]

64

"Black bees emerging
from the blooming lotus
are like specks of fragrant betel
spat from the mouth of a drowsy woman
awakening at dawn.

65

"The doors of darkness creaked
as the charioteer of the Sun forced them open,
the Water Lily clucked
as she lulled her babies to sleep,
the Mandeha demons roared like lions
as they blocked the path of the Sun.
You can hear all these sounds
in the rooster's call at dawn.

66

"When the king, the Moon, decamped,
his soldiers, the stars, set fire
to the camp, the night sky.
The flames burning red
are the colors of dawn
rising in the east.

67

"Birds in their nests on trees near the lake
flapped their wings—*paṭa-paṭa-paṭa*—
as if the Women of the Directions
were snapping their fingers
when their friend, Lotus, yawned.[18]

68

"The night sky has cleared up; the world is bathed in light.
The moon and the lips of women kissed by their lovers—
　　both have lost their color.

Everything in the world is clearly seen, the peaks of the
    Eastern Mountain as well.
The upper stories of tall buildings are unfolding like a
    lotus, brilliant and fragrant.
The planets have disappeared, and calves, untied, run
    away.
Meditating Brahmans have closed their eyes, silent like
    sleeping owls.

69

"As the rays of the sun grew hotter and hotter,
the queen water lily, unable to bear the heat,
covered herself in her petals,
That's how it is—
kings' women never see the sun.[19]

70

"Coaxed by the soft words of Dawn
sung by birds flying from their nests—
the *gogu* flowers on the eastern hill
blossomed in a bunch.[20]
That's why the eastern sky is crimson at sunrise."

71

Krishna woke up to the sweet words of the morning sing-
ers. He finished his morning routine and entered the court
along with Brahmans, elders, and ministers. He bowed to his
teachers Ugrasena, Vasudeva, and Balabhadra; greeted his
brothers Satyaki and Sarana; acknowledged the salutations
of princes Pradyumna, Samba, and Aniruddha; paid respect

to the families of Yadava, Vrishni, Bhoja, and Andhaka; and sat on his throne and gestured to everyone to take their seats. Eager to accomplish the tasks of the day, Krishna quickly summoned Garuda,

72

the eagle
who fought off Indra and his diamond *vajra* by throwing a
    single feather,[21]
who feasted on an elephant and a tortoise in preparation
    for battle with Indra,[22]
the ideal son who freed his mother from slavery,
who stole the nectar of immortality from the gods,
the beloved brother of the sun's charioteer,
the fruit of his father's good deeds,
the supreme king of the empire of birds,
obsessed with hunting snakes,
whose feathers decorate Vishnu's arrow shot by Shiva at
    the Three Cities,[23]
who broke the branch of the great tree *rohiṇa*,[24]
who flies faster than thought—
Garuda came.

73

Landing on the earth from the sky, Garuda, son of Vinata, was so heavy that he made the heads of the First Snake bend low.[25] He humbly bowed to Krishna's feet.

74

Krishna told him the whole story:
how Narada came and gave him a flower, which he gave to
     Rukmini;
how a servant secretly carried word to Satyabhama;
how jealous Satya became angry;
how Krishna begged her;
and how he made this promise to her.

75

Garuda was happy. "Krishna," he said, "this is like a gift to
me. Indra has been angry with me from the day I deflected
his *vajra*. He has still not forgotten. This gives me a chance
to get even."

76

"Indeed, you can do that," said Krishna to Garuda. Krishna
summoned his relatives and friends. He told them of his
journey and asked them to protect the city in his absence.
Taking leave of them, he mounted the bird, together with
Satyabhama.

77

Garuda flew through the sky toward Indra's city, carrying
Krishna and his beloved Satyabhama, flying faster than
thought. Rows of clouds were cast aside like wisps of cotton
by the wind from his strong wings.

78

Krishna's weapons,
discus, club, bow, and conch,
flew with him on either side,
and the conch began to blow
from the wind stirred up by Garuda's wings,
announcing Krishna's journey.

79

Dew drops from the clouds
adorned Satyabhama's hair,
as if the goddess Sky
had given her a gift
of a glistening string of pearls.

80

Dark clouds flashed with lightning, sapphire parasols with
golden handles held over Krishna.

81

The dark streaks of Krishna's body flying in the sky looked
like the waters of Yamuna, the dark river, rushing to meet
her father, the Sun.[26]

82

Unable to bear the harsh wind from Garuda's wings, the
snakes that tie the Sun's horses to the yoke hid under the
chariot. The chariot froze. Aruna, the charioteer, quickly
tied them back together and sped off into the sky, without
losing time.

83

Flying past this chariot, Garuda bowed to his older brother,
Aruna, who blessed him, even as he was flying. Krishna and
Satya applauded their feats.

84

As they went beyond the path of the sky riding on Garuda,
Krishna, skilled in words, spoke with a smile to Satyabhama.
She listened, her sparkling eyes wide open.

85

"Look at Mount Meru, a feast for the eyes.
Like another Garuda,
it shines with an armor of gold
struck by Indra's *vajra*.[27]
The sun and moon circle the mountain just for fun,
keeping watch in turns.

86

"Here, on this divine mountain,
cuckoos see jewels on the hoods of snakes
    coiled around trees in autumn,
        think they are young shoots, and try to eat them.
Wild buffalos see a mirage of water
        created by melting moonstones,
            lunge at it, and break their horns.
Bears think the golden light from precious topaz
        is real honey and lick it.

Lions think the smooth sapphire boulders
    are dark elephants
    and break their claws pouncing at them.
Deer see grass in emerald stones and, to reach it,
jump over forest fires that are really rubies.

87

"Look at the Chenchu women.[28]
Waiting for moonrise, they lie in ambush,
then come close and shoot the deer,
but it doesn't die.[29]
They think they missed their mark,
not knowing that the deer drinks
the nectar of life from the moon.
They throw down their bows and arrows
and wander the slopes in shame.

88

"Among the boulders of Meru, the golden mountain, huge elephants rub against each other, and their ichor floods the surrounding area. Gandharva women use that ichor as ink to write love letters on palm leaves that the forest goddesses use for earrings.

Young peacocks see the reflection of large snakes from the underworld appearing on the raised crystals of the mountain and cast aside their small prey. They pierce the reflection with their beaks, strike it with the tips of their wings, and kick it with their feet. Watching those peacocks puffed up with anger from these vain attempts, Garuda women point them out to their husbands and laugh.

Mountain streams, sizzling from sunstones hot from the midday sun, mix with civet that settles as a rim around the edges of the water. Flowers fall into the water from trees shaken by troupes of leaping monkeys. Yaksha women bathe in that perfumed water and relax their bodies, tired from making love.

Slender Sadhya women string necklaces of pearls that fell
      in one place from:
conch and oyster shells amid the clouds,
clouds scattered by stalks of bamboo,
bamboo broken by the sharp fangs of a boar,
the boar wandering in pain from the blow of an elephant,
the elephant slashed on his temples by a young lion.[30]

The snakes circling the edges of the mountain in search
      of food look like leeches healing Mount Meru's
      open wounds caused by Indra when he cut off the
      mountain's wings with his *vajra*.[31]

Tigers sleep on enormous rocks, a carpet of precious gems spread out for the assembly of the gods.

Packs of white-mouthed bears wander around looking like
      Rahu, who had eaten half the moon.[32]

Meru Mountain is:[33]

thick with a scented breeze from trees such as *śakra, pura, mahiḷa,*[34] lime, and sandalwood— listen well: my words could also mean it is like Indra's court, filled with fragrance from the perfume on the breasts of Amaravati's women;

covered with dark, brown grass and jacktrees on small hills and narrow valleys—it may also appear like the ocean across which heroes from the Ramayana, Nila, Nala, and Panasa, built a bridge;

beautiful with shoots of *kakubha* trees—you may also think it's like a vina with a beautiful head and handle;[35]

delightful with segments, *parva,* of bamboo—or it may be like the hundred chapters, *parva,* of the epic Mahabharata;

filled with wandering elephants—it also looks like a battleground with a fourfold army that includes elephants;[36]

shining with groups of colored metals, *dhātu*—or it could be like classes of roots, *dhātu,* of words in grammar;

filled with Nishada hunters—it may also sound like music with the seventh note, *niṣāda.*

On that mountain:[37]

> its peaks block the clouds—rivers flow from its crest;

> mountain buffaloes roam—but then, trees and birds reside there too;

> sounds of the bamboo resonate—you may also hear young deer roaming.

89

"Sweet-voiced lady,
look at those sweet-voiced Kinnara couples.
Drunk with honey from the wish-giving tree,
they sing songs in honor of Indra
in high-pitched voices,
plucking their Kinnara lutes
on the peaks of Mount Meru.

90

"Look at those Siddha travelers.
They eat their packed meals
with curds from the gods' cow
on leaves from the birch tree,
rest awhile in the cool shade of the *kalpa* tree,
playing and joking,
and move on to Mount Kailasa.

91

"There are the Vidyadharas who meditate on Shiva.
Look at their jeweled earrings, their daggers,
the vinas they strum in their hands,
their turbans, white as moonlight,
match the lines of ash on their foreheads
and the big pearls hanging from their necks.

92

"Here are the Gandharvas,
experts in singing songs
taught by the goddess of music herself.
They travel in flying chariots,
have horse heads,[38]
accompany the dances of Apsarasas,
and live where Yakshas live.

93

"See all these people on their way to entertain Indra—
Yakshas, banding together to sing in the court of the gods;
Guhyas, masters of comedy and friends of Bhringi;*
Garudas, friends of Vishvaksena† and dear to Garuda
    himself;
Charanas, skilled in storytelling and travelers of the
    world—
they are all surprised to see us here today.

---

* Attendant of Shiva.
† Attendant of Vishnu.

94

"See the Ganga, Jahnu's daughter,
dancing on the head of Shiva.
When the sons of Sagara were burned
by the fiery looks of Kapila,
she became the stairway
to the pinnacle of their release.[39]
She flows across the three worlds:
heaven, earth, and the world below.
She is Yamuna's dear friend,
and here she embraces the Kanakhala mountain.

95

"These are the houses of the sages,
playgrounds for deer raised on
the same tender leaves of grass that adorn
the ears of the sages' wives, Anasuya and Arundhati.
Swaths of bark cloth from the giving tree
decorate their doorways,
and smoke from the three Vedic fires
turns the area a charming gray.

96

"Do you see the heavenly cow, Kamadhenu?
She rose from the milk-ocean after
the celestial dancers, the nectar of immortality,
the tree of wishes, the moon,
and the wishing stone—
better than all that came before her.[40]

She lies on a grassy bed, chewing cud,
licking the neck of her daughter, Nandini.

97

"Woman with eyes of a young deer,
see that fortress at a distance.
It is like a headband tied across the forehead
of the king of Mount Meru,
and Vaijayanta, this city of gods,
his crown.

98

"Look at the gods' chariots,
adorned with silk flags flapping in the wind,
appearing as if other cities are bowing down,
unable to match the power of
this city of Indra, king of gods.

99

"Heroes who fought in battle without a trace of fear,
Brahmans who perform sacrifices strictly by the book,
sages who break the bonds of existence—
all feel fulfilled by a single kiss
from even one heavenly woman.

100

"A good man reaches this city,
like a good sailor navigating the ocean of life, evading
the eyes of women, sharp as sharks,

the mountains that are their breasts,
and whirlpools of infatuation.
Only he can reach this island city."

101

Krishna, his mind lost in happiness, described that great city
to Satyabhama as they climbed the peaks of Mount Meru.

102

Garuda landed on the peak,
showing his expert maneuvers—
bhañjalika, murali, and *sudhāla.*[41]
Astonished, the gods moved aside
and bowed in wonder.
Krishna smiled at them
and walked along the path on the banks of Ganga
marked with hoof prints of the gods' cow Kamadhenu,
shaped like the eye of a peacock feather.

103

They soothed their weary bodies
with the fragrant breeze that carried
the sounds of geese
chewing on sweet lotus stalks,
again and again.

104

Krishnadevaraya,
capable of tireless fighting,
you are Brihaspati in intellect,

like Indra's vajra *cast at warriors,*
and like Vishnu, protector of the world.
You destroyed the cities Ummatturu and Shivamsamudra
in the middle of the river Kaveri,
invincible like Lanka, the city of the ten-headed demon,
in the middle of the ocean.

105

Husband of Tirumaladevi,
your heart flows with compassion,
king of kings,
son of Ishvaranarasa,
you are known by the title, "One of Unbreakable Promises."

106

Son of Narasimha, husband of Nagamba,
you excel even Indra in your life of pleasure,
endless treasury filled with the wealth of giving,
you rule the earth bounded by the sea.

Timmaya of the Kaushika lineage,
Singaya's son, blessed by Shiva with poetic skill,
composed this great poem, Theft of a Tree.
This is its second chapter.

Chapter 3

1

Shri lives in your palace,
Krishnaraya,
destroyer of the Utkala kings,
crown jewel of the lunar family,
every woman's dream. [1]

2

Vaishampayana to Janamejaya:

Krishna and Satyabhama arrived on the banks of the Ganga.

3

When Narada informed Indra of Krishna's impending arrival, he hurriedly mounted Airavata and rushed to meet him, filled with excitement. Indra's son Jayanta, the lords of the directions, and Menaka and other courtesans accompanied him. [2]

4

Indra, the god of gods, saw Krishna at a distance and prodded his elephant to kneel. He dismounted from the elephant, landing on the tips of his toes. Indra tied his upper cloth around his waist and bowed low, his crown grazing the earth.

5

Tears of joy streaming down his face,
his body bristling with excitement,
Indra, alive with love,
touched Krishna's feet.
Drawn to the flowers on Indra's crown,
bees buzzed,
gently asking after Krishna's welfare.

6

Indra's eyes blossomed with delight,
as if offering Krishna new lotuses.
The killer of demons stretched forth his dark arms
and embraced the king of Amaravati,
a new monsoon cloud
hugging the peaks of a tall mountain.

7

Agni folded his hands,
Yama prostrated,
Nirruti kneeled,
Varuna paid his respects,
Vayu joined his palms together,
Kubera bowed,
Ishana, the moon in his crown, knelt before
the best of the Yadavas—
the lords of the directions were thrilled.

8

The discus-bearer acknowledged each of them with playful words and smiling looks and beckoned Indra to mount his elephant. Relieved of the fatigue of travel by the cool breeze fanned by courtesans, Rambha and Tara, Krishna ascended Garuda.

9

Each of the gods mounted his vehicle. The sounds of drums and cymbals filled the sky, as if the sky itself was shouting with joy.

10

Indra cleared the path, asking Siddhas, Kimpurushas, Yakshas, and Vasus to step aside and give way. Krishna, his body dark as *atasi* flowers, flew through the sky, to the amazement of Narada and other sages.[3]

11

The city's women, all aflutter, rushed
to see Krishna,
their ornaments mismatched in haste.
They pushed each other away,
each wanting to be in front,
as they ran up to the rooftops
of the city's shimmering palaces.

12

A woman asked her friend:
"Why smear yourself with sandal paste
when it will smudge
the moment you see Hari?
Tears of joy will dissolve the kohl in your eyes,
and the designs on your cheeks will fade
from the tingling of your skin.
Forget about adorning yourself."

13

Another woman came late
and seeing no place at the window,
she urgently called away her young friend,
on some excuse,
then quickly took her place
to watch Krishna.
The other women laughed,
clapping their hands,
at the trick she'd played.

14

A woman just out of her bath
came running, eager to see Krishna.
Her long hair
damp with fragrant sandal water
fell across her breasts.
She held it up in her hands
as she hurried along the royal path,

as if carrying a gift of a peacock's tail
for Gopala.

15

A woman, her waist so thin it was hardly there,
climbed to the palace terrace to see Krishna,
her body tingling with desire.
When her friends caught sight of her,
she lied, "Can't you see I'm tired?"

16

"Don't others want to see him too?"
said a woman to her co-wife.
"You're a great beauty,
you know all sorts of tricks.
In the end, he'll see no one but you."

17

A woman, her hair black as bees,
was beside herself seeing Krishna,
the knot of her sari came loose,
but the cloth stayed in place,
stuck to the sweat of her body.
Puffed rice fell by itself
on Krishna's head
from her trembling hands.
She was lucky—
love came to her aid.

18

A woman distracted by Krishna
wore her anklet around her wrist.
As her body swelled with desire
the anklet shattered into tiny pieces.

19

A slender woman scattered puffed rice
on Krishna, killer of demons.
As if jealous,
her braid spilled a spray of flowers,
her eyes sprinkled tears of joy,
her forehead shed beads of sweat,
and her breasts dropped strings of pearls
broken by the burst of passion.

20

A woman, voice sweet as a parrot's,
taught her own parrot to call, "Krishna, come here."
With the glance of an eye,
Krishna pointed her out to Satyabhama.
The other woman glared at him,
eyes flashing with anger.

21

The windows of Amaravati were filled with women.
The hearts of those women were filled with desire.
Krishna became that desire.

22

Krishna listened to all those women sneering at each other,
hungry to see him. Smiling to himself, he dismounted Garuda
and crossed the royal grounds to Indra's palace. Guards with
jeweled staffs yelled out, and all space resounded with their
shouts.

23

Indra welcomed Krishna, taking his hand with affection.
Together, they walked through all three courtyards, guarded
by elephants keeping watch, and arrived at the palace.

24

Krishna saw Aditi sitting comfortably
on a pedestal studded with jewels
near a bed of *kalpa* flowers.
Her feet were stretched out on the thighs of Shachi,
    who was massaging them gently.
Sitting at her side, Sarasvati, jewel among women,
    was telling her stories.
The wives of the seven sages
    walked about, ready to serve her.
The wives of the lords of the directions
    held trays of betel leaves, fans, and whisks.
Aditi is the mother of all gods,
born like pearls from an oyster.

25

Along with Satya, Krishna bowed to Aditi and gave her the earrings that he took from Naraka, untying them from the fold of his golden upper cloth. Delighted, Aditi blessed him and beckoned him to sit on a seat adorned with precious jewels.

26

She patted his back and kissed his forehead. "Enemy of demons," she said, "I must be really fortunate to see you. You are not easy to reach, even for the sages who meditate on you. I am now free of flaws.

27

"As Brahma, you bring about creation.
As Vishnu, you sustain the world with compassion.
As Shiva, you devour it again—
all this is part of your play
and yet, you are beyond it all.
You hold a discus as an ornament on your strong arm,
how can I praise you?[4]

28

"When you took the form of a fish and struck the water with your tail, the mountains in the ocean felt the blows of Indra's *vajra* a second time. With your sharp fin and tail, you cut down the demon who stole the Vedas and returned them to Brahma, the god born from a lotus.

29

"When gods and demons became friends, both wanting the elixir of life, they fastened the king of snakes as a rope on Mount Mandara. When they started churning the ocean of milk, the mountain sank. Didn't you take the shape of a tortoise to support it? You even tricked the demons, deluding them as Mohini, the most beautiful woman in the world.

30

"When the earth sank into the ocean at the end of time, you took the form of a boar and dug down to the underworld. You lifted it up on the edge of your tusks, god who sleeps on the Primordial Snake.

31

"The enormous pot that is the universe showed cracks, and the earth sank deep into the ocean where crocodiles crawl. You came in the form of a huge boar and lifted the tender Earth with your white tusk—a black bee drawn to the tip of a white *ketaka* flower.[5]

32

"'Stop being clever! You say Hari is everywhere. Can you show him here, in this pillar?' When the demon Hiranyakashipu challenged his son, you came as Narasimha, cracked open the pillar, and tore apart the demon's chest with your sharp claws.

33

"You wanted to make me luckier than my co-wife, Diti, when you were born as my son, Vamana.[6] You stomped on Bali with your feet high as the sky. The sun became your footstool, and its rays radiated out like filaments from your lotus feet.

34

"Swinging your ax with your invincible arms, you pulverized clans of royal warriors. With the same ax, you carved a hole in Mount Krauncha, making a path for royal geese to descend to earth. You slashed the arms of Kartavirya, your enemy. You shot an arrow at the ocean and made yourself a home. You are famous as Parashurama.[7]

35

"When your wife, the most beautiful woman in the world, was stolen, you led an army of monkeys, bridged the ocean, and cut off Ravana's ten heads. The flood of your fame washed away the mud that was the shame of Mount Kailasa.[8] You are Rama, the great Raghu king.

36

"You killed the demon Pralamba and you redirected Yamuna, the black river. To save your son, you uprooted Hastinapura with the edge of your plow, terrifying all the Kaurava warriors. You are the husband of Revati, the famous Balarama.

37

"You came as the false Buddha and seduced the chaste wives of the Three Cities, making them weak with desire. You threw their invincible husbands into the fire from Shiva's third eye. Your eyes are fully awake to save the world.

38

"Best of Yadavas!⁹ Brahma, the creator of the three worlds, lives in the lotus rising from your navel. You are illumined by the rays from the Kaustubha gem on your chest, a footrest for Lakshmi. The heavenly Ganga springs from your feet and washes away the dust from Shiva's matted locks. You dwell in the hearts of sages who stay still, deep in meditation, with the drops of life flowing from the mouth of the snake Kundalini. The sages control their breath, moving it through the six chakras of their bodies and loosening the three knots: *jālandhara, uḍyāṇa,* and *mūla.*¹⁰

When the gods came with Brahma and begged you to protect the earth, you were born from Devaki's womb. At birth, you showed Devaki your five weapons—sword, discus, conch, mace, and bow—in your four arms.¹¹ You revealed to her your yellow garments and your chest, adorned by Lakshmi. Seeing all of this, Devaki was afraid and begged for protection, saying: '*Kāvu, kāvu!* Protect me, protect me!' Then you, a small child, began to cry, '*Kāvu, kāvu!*'¹²

When your father moved you to the cowherd village, the demon Putana came there, disguised as a cowherd woman, wanting to suckle you on her poisonous milk. You clasped her breast, round like a conch blown at the time of her death, and sucked out her life-breath.

You kicked the demon who was in the form of a cart and destroyed him. When you kept stealing butter, the gopis complained to your mother Yashoda. 'What kind of a child are you?' your mother yelled and bound you to a mortar. You dragged the mortar through two big *maddi* trees and felled them.[13] And still you made everyone think you were only a child.

In the woods of Brindavana, where calves and herders roamed, you were luminous, peacock feathers tucked into your hair, wearing a necklace of *guñja* beads, a flute in your hand.[14] When Brahma stole the cows and the herders and hid them away, you took the form of all of them, shattering Brahma's pride.

It was a game: when you danced on the hood of Kaliya as though it were a stage, to the sound of the resounding waves of the rushing Kalindi.

The wives of the sages secretly gave you and the other cowherd children the food that their husbands had saved for the gods. You gave them the gift of liberation in return.

When a demon-snake swallowed all the cows and herders, you entered his mouth and tore him in half to save everyone.

You stopped the cowherds from worshiping Indra and took the offerings for yourself. Furious, Indra sent down rain like a shower of arrows, as rocks and mountains tumbled. The cowherds began to flee in fear, but then you raised up Govardhana, sheltering them under it.

As an elephant in rut lifts up a delicate lotus flower, you caught hold of the demon who had the form of the bull Arishta and crushed him. When the horse-demon Keshi attacked you, you pushed your arm into his mouth and sucked out his life-breath.[15]

You stood on the Yamuna's sandy bank, luminous in the bright autumn moonlight, a flute touching your lips, your brows arched, your head slightly cocked. As you played the flute, cows stopped chewing cud, the Yamuna slowed, and withered trees near a waterless pond suddenly bloomed. The gopis and Radha, drawn to the fifth note of your flute, ran to you, beside themselves with passion. You made them float on an ocean of happiness with your love games.

Your uncle Kamsa heard of your strength in defeating impossible demons and wanted to see you for himself. He sent his minister Akrura to invite you. When you met Akrura on the way, you showed him your cosmic form, beyond thought. Akrura became your devotee, and you accepted him as yours. You entered Kamsa's capital, making him anxious with fear. When a dwarf woman with a twisted body gave you sandal paste as a gift, you embraced her and lifted her up, transforming her into a beautiful woman.

You broke the bow worshiped by Kamsa and beheaded the army of guards protecting it. You entered his court loud with the defiant cries of arm-slapping wresters, thundering drums, and the yells of soldiers ready for a fight.[16] When the elephant driver incited the royal elephant at the entrance of the court, you killed it and applied the ichor of the elephant as a mark on your forehead, wore the pearls from its temples as earrings, smeared its thick blood on your body, wielded its tusk as a mace in your hand. You caught hold of the leg of the wrestler Chanura, whirled him around, and destroyed him. The demon-king Kamsa, struck with fear, tried to escape, but you wrestled him and crushed the neck of the plague of the three worlds.

The gods played melodious instruments in celebration, and flowers from the tree of wishes fell from the heavens. To the delight of the world, you consecrated Ugrasena as the heir to Kamsa's kingdom.[17]

Through Bhima, you ordered the death of the arrogant Jarasandha with his eightfold army. When you had Yudhishthira conduct the royal consecration, Shishupala spoke ill of you because you are not of royal warrior birth. Shishupala protested with pride and arrogance because the first ritual offering was given to you, so you lifted your discus and cut off his head. With the same discus, you struck Paundra, the false Vasudeva. You fought the armies of Kumara and Ganesha, chased Shiva, cut Bana's thousand arms, and saved the world.[18]

Vanquisher of terrible Naraka, Draupadi's protector, you revived Sandipa's son to end a father's grief at the death of his son. The branches of the Vedas blossom from your feet. Here, you are Krishna, Satyabhama's beloved."

39

Having praised him with this garland of words, Aditi said: "You contain the whole universe. Please stay here with your wife for a few days, let me serve you." Krishna bowed to her, the mother of all the gods, accepted her invitation, and turned to Indra.[19]

40

Indra came forward and said, "Enjoy Vaijayanta, my palace." Krishna smiled and took Indra's hands in his own. While Ishana and the other lords of the directions served him, Krishna toured that superb palace.

41

Vaijayanta was truly resplendent.

Garlands of golden lotuses from the celestial Ganga made it sparkle.

It was surrounded on all sides by flying chariots tinkling with golden bells, which sounded like its own children chattering sweetly.

Chintamani adorned its highest point, reflecting every desire, suggesting the palace itself was a storehouse of wishes.

The rows of windows studded with sapphires looked like Shri's sidelong glances.

All the gods of the palace, refined in their taste, gathered to relish the graceful dance of hundreds of celestial Apsarasas, which were mirrored in the shimmering jeweled pillars of the palace.

The walls were filled with paintings proclaiming the heroic feats of Indra, king of gods, who killed the demons Puloma, Namuchi, Jambha, Paka, Vritra, Bala, and others.

The white crystal of the palace reflected everything, and Indra's elephant Airavata and his horse Ucchaishravas resting there appeared as if they were taking a bath in the ocean of milk.[20]

The divine architect's mechanical dolls carried fineries such as jeweled pots, boxes for betel nut, palm-leaf fans, yak-tail fans, mirrors, platters, and sandalwood, confusing the female servants, who were supposed to carry the same.

The flowing waves of the celestial Ganga seemed to be responding to the invitation of the fluttering flags of white silk made from the leaves of the wish-giving tree.[21]

Gardeners cooled jeweled porches with *mandāra*-scented water.[22]

At the front of the house, golden cots were placed on raised platforms. Young shoots of another *kalpa* tree were placed on the cots, giving an impression of the crimson colors of dusk.[23]

White silk canopies perfumed with the dust of fragrant pollen from *kalpa* flowers appeared like moonlight.

Shachi, Indra's wife, made offerings from *pārijāta* flowers, which were mirrored on the jeweled floors of that palace like constellations of stars. Flames of the fire offering lit by Agni's wife, Svaha, shone on golden plates. Yama's wife, Dhumorna, placed sandalwood and aloe, which gave off fragrant smoke. Nirruti's wife made ritual offerings appropriate for the first entry into the house. Varuna's wife made forest garlands from the young shoots of beautiful coral vines. Vayu's wife appointed young girls to wave fans laced with scented camphor. Kubera's wife arranged golden decorations in the shapes of a conch, lotus, and crocodile.[24] Vaijayanta was a feast for the eyes.[25]

Krishna entered the palace along with Satyabhama. He bade farewell to Indra, Agni, Yama, Nirruti, Varuna, Vayu, Kubera, and Ishana, and rested there.

42

Krishna, Balarama's dear brother, said to Satyabhama:
"Woman with eyes bright as lotuses, let's take a look at
the garden of the gods." Excited, they set out and arrived
at the banks of the heavenly river. Celestial courtesans—
Ghritachi, Menaka, Manjughosha, Rambha, and Harini—
followed them.

43

A soft breeze arose from
the flapping of the wings of bees
drunk on the spray of honey
dripping from sandal and *pārijāta* trees
in the garden of the gods.

44

Krishna, the lifter of Govardhana,
wandered Indra's garden with his beloved wife and saw:
a *kuravaka,* that blossoms with the embrace of Rambha's
    round breasts
a *campaka,* with the glimmer of Manjughosha's lotus face
a *kesara,* with the honey wine spit from Harini's mouth
a *kaṅkeḷi,* from a kick by Urvashi's feet freshly decorated
    with lac
a *sinduvāra,* by the gentle breeze from Menaka's fragrant
    breath.[26]
All the trees that blossom in different seasons
flower here at the same time.

45

"Krishna and his beloved wife Satya are visiting the garden
of Indra, destroyer of mountains, accompanied by the gods'
women." Hearing the news, the seasons—monsoon, autumn,
frost, winter, spring, and summer—went to the royal garden
to honor him.

46

At one place, monsoon staged a dance of lightning
    in a theater of thundering rain clouds.
In another place, autumn presented collections of
    cackling geese gathered in lotus ponds.
And then there were frosty sprays of perfumed mist
    from newly blossoming *cāmanti* flowers.[27]
Winter displayed a luxuriant coolness
    from the fragrance of *preṅkana* and clove trees.
A spring breeze spread from Mount Malaya,
moist with the waters of Tamraparni.
The garden was filled with newly opened
summer flowers: jasmine, *pāṭali, campaka,* and water lily.

47

The mango vine's fine shoots
are the line down a woman's navel,
and its leaves, brushed by the breeze from Sandalwood
    Mountain,
drop like jewels shed by a pregnant woman,
too weary to wear them.

48

The white flowers on the mango tree's red shoots
were her teeth biting into her lips in anger
as Spring made love to the *gurivĕnda* vine,
the other woman.

49

A cuckoo tore apart a cluster of new shoots with its beak, as
if proclaiming to Manmatha, "This is how I'll rip the hearts
of lovers tormented by separation."

50

The long, lovely vines that dropped their leaves
when touched by the breeze from Mount Malaya
reminded Krishna of the innocent gopis
who shyly slipped into the river,
dropping their clothes on the shore.[28]

51

Bees scrape their noses, hoping to taste
  honey from young mango flowers not yet open.
They try to eat mango shoots, find the taste astringent,
  and wash their mouths with water
  flavored by *gŏjjega* flowers.[29]
They see *goraṇṭa* flowers hidden behind *campakas* and
  avoid them in fear, still watering in their mouths.
They go toward *kaligŏṭṭu* flowers not yet in bloom
  and turn back, frustrated, to the jasmine flowers
  they are used to.

Young bees are all over the garden
wherever you look,
like the vanguard of the love god—
the garden is truly a feast for the eyes.

52

The garden has the joys of all seasons in one place. Nanda's
son, Krishna, wandered about Nandana garden, attended by
the gods' women, and said to his beloved wife:

53

"It looks like the newlywed couple—the beautiful bride
Garden and handsome Spring—were pouring rice on each
other at their wedding. See the ground covered in buds from
the areca tree.

54

"Look at those betel vines
like delicate women.
The streaks of juice that fell on their tender leaves
when parrots pecked at the fruit above
are designs painted by Spring
on their glowing cheeks.
And you know something else?
Your dark hair is darker than bees.

55

"Woman, your waist is so thin it can't be seen.
Those pomegranate seeds
that fell from the beaks of drunken parrots
look like ladybugs that appear
when trees clustering like clouds
shower down streams of honey.

56

"Wife, did you see that?
The cuckoo tried to grab
the tender lips of the mango vine,
who pushed him away with a shake of her hand,
bracelets tinkling.
You can hear it in the sounds of the bees.

57

"Look at that desperate female bee
falling into a flood of *campaka* fragrance.
She has caught her husband
with another female
sipping honey from a different flower.
Her friends, even her husband, beg
her to stop.
Burning in anger,
she won't listen.
I know all too well—
a woman can be very determined."

58

Krishna put his arm around Satya's shoulders, and together they wandered among the trees. The goddess of the garden honored them, sprinkling them with honey from *aśoka* flowers, then drying it with fine cloth from the *kalpa* tree.

59

Krishnaraya,
your valor is unbearable as the scorching sun to your enemies,
you are a great giver,
you rule the earth encircled by all four oceans,
because you worship Vishnu, enemy of demons,
the lands extending to the ends of the earth
are brightened by the light of your fame,
women all over the world fall in love with you,
you are more handsome than Love, the moon, and Jayanta,*
you have an artistic mind.

60

King of kings,
the land near Udayagiri and Kondavidu is covered
with crushed pearls from the temples of elephants
that form the army of the Kalinga king.

61

The river Kaveri flows red
from the blood streaming down the necks
of your enemies, slain on its banks.

---

* Indra's son.

It is like a woman flowing in search of her lover, the ocean.
Your battle drums sound like huge mountains
shattering under the force of Indra's vajra.

Timmaya of the Kaushika lineage,
Singaya's son, blessed by Shiva with poetic skill,
composed this great poem, Theft of a Tree.
This is its third chapter.

Chapter 4

1

Krishnaraya,
devoted to serving the god of Venkata hills,
beloved husband of Cinnamadevi,
in praising the skill of poets,
you are like the thousand-tongued lord of snakes.[1]

2

"Listen," Vaishampayana said to Janamejaya.

As Krishna and Satyabhama wandered the garden, they saw
the *pārijāta* tree and were excited.

3

Krishna looked at Satya,
"My dear, do you see this *pārijāta?*
The three worlds praise the fragrance
of the king of trees,
heaven's only ornament,
like the moon in Shiva's hair
and the Kaustubha on Vishnu's chest.

4

"The gentle breeze that blows through
the silk hanging from its branches
comforts Shachi's maids,
the courtesans of the gods,
tired from collecting its flowers.

5

"Look at the swarm of young bees tricked into drinking
light from the tree's dazzling flowers, thinking it is fragrant
honey; they're thirsty—you can see their long beaks trem-
bling and hear the buzzing of their wings.

6

"If they didn't hear them calling, the gods' women wouldn't
ever see the birds hidden among the tree's ornaments.

7

"The whole tree is reflected in the water around its trunk, as
if it's plunging down to earth even before we take it there.

8

"Every day with immense pleasure,
Indra seats his beloved wife Shachi on his lap,
straightens her tangled hair,
makes a garland of flowers from this tree
with a string of lotus stalks,
and wraps it around her bun.

9

"The gods' women only have to think of
any tree they want it to be—
tilaka, campaka, krovi, sinduvāra, preṅkana,
māmiḍi, gogu, pŏnna, pŏgaḍa, and *kaṅkeḷi*—
and do the *dohada* act suitable to each tree—
glancing, looking up, embracing, smelling, singing,
stroking, talking, laughing, spitting liquor, and kicking.[2]
The flowers of all those trees
appear on this one.

10

"A *tilaka* gives flowers when Apsarasas look at it,
kesara when they spit liquor on it,
preṅkana when they sing for it,
māvi when they stroke it,
pŏnna when they laugh at it,
campaka when they lift their face to it,
and *kŏravi* when they embrace it,
for the *vāvili,* they have to smell it,
for the *aśoka,* they have to kick it,
they have to speak to the *gogu.*
This one tree gives all those flowers
by these acts alone."[3]

11

"Why delay?" said Satyabhama to her husband.
"Stay true to your word,
respected all over the world,
uproot this tree
and plant it behind my house.
Make me happy,
lord of my life."

12

The killer of Kaitabha smiled. "Let's stroll around the garden
a little longer, attended by these women of heaven. Then
I'll do what you want," he said, tucking a cluster of *pārijāta*
flowers behind her ear.

13

He comforted Satya, the love of his life,
and together they wandered Indra's garden.
Excited, he plucked flowers
with the tips of his nails
sharpened on gopis' breasts,
round as a bunch of flowers.

14

Young bees swarmed around
the eyes of the gods' women,
mistaking them for black lotuses.
Being women from heaven, they couldn't blink,
and their hands weren't big enough to cover their eyes.

Annoyed, they looked enviously at Satyabhama,
who closed her eyes in fear,
and wished they were human, too.

15

Joking among themselves, the women collected flowers.
They moved carefully by the edges of the beds of pollen
so they would not step on Krishna's footprints, marked by
auspicious signs.[4]

16

"Friend, what's the hurry? Pluck the *goraṇṭa* with the tip
    of your nail."[5]
"Gently sprinkle water on the lotuses, they're frail."

"You've hit the vine so sharply, it's hurting."
"Look at the mynah. Her lover is coming to see her, she's
    rejoicing."

"Don't sulk. Take those jasmine flowers and tuck them in
    your bun."
"You hate to share. That's no fun."

"You placed a bet. I brought *preṅkana* flowers because I
    can sing."
"You made this choker with *pŏnna* flowers. It's a nice
    string."

"Friend, you're greedy. Don't ask for these flowers from
    me."

"Your hair is filled with pollen. Wipe it with honey from
the mango tree."

"That's no way to speak to the *pŏnna*. You have to laugh
with it."
"Don't pluck those flowers. They're only open a bit."

"Stop turning the garlands over and over. The flowers are
twisted out of shape."
"Go away! These mango trees are ours, they're our
escape."

"Don't use that language. You called me a child when I
talk."
"You caught that goose, mimicking it with your slow
walk."

"Hey Ghritachi, did you kick the *aśoka?* Its fragrance
spreads everywhere."
"Rambha, you're calling me for honey. Among the
bananas there's plenty to share."

"You lied to me when I asked for flowers. Don't touch my
large lime."
"You love this vine more than your life. Don't step on it
this time."

"Manjughosha, this golden vine in the gods' garden is
nothing rare."

"This vine is not afraid of bees. We know that, but we
    don't care."

"Parrots drank the mango juice and they're wildly
    talking."
"We pluck the mango shoots and hear the cuckoos
    flocking."

"This woman can reach the fragrant *mŏgali* with her
    hook."
"Don't be stubborn. The *gŏjjagi* are too far even to take a
    look."[6]

17

The women played,
rocking on swings made of vines,
plucking the centers from golden lotuses,
throwing pollen on each other.
As they wandered about the garden,
the sun rose to the middle of the sky,
its rays harsh beyond bearing.

18

The knots of their saris came loose,
their faces wilted,
hair undone,
designs on their cheeks smeared,
necklaces tangled,
sighs heavy,

eyes red with pollen,
the women looked weary
as if from making love.

19

Their stalks wilted from the hot sun,
flowers drooped,
looking like fragrant beads of sweat
on the body of the Garden Goddess.

20

Snakes lay down in hunger for lack of a cool breeze,[7]
bees were scared to drink the boiling honey from lotus
    blooms,
golden boulders on the slopes of Mount Meru melted,
afraid of cranes, fish hid in the thick mud of dried-up
    ponds.

21

Their eyes motionless,
wings dangling loose,
breasts leaning on branches,
parched mouths open,
breath heavy,
necks inflamed—
birds scorched by the midday sun
hung in the trees
calling out to friends
in feeble voices.

22

To quench the thirst of his mate,
a lovebird flapped his wings
to cool the boiling honey,
then through a lotus stalk
fed it to her drop by drop.

23

To cool her from the heat of the sun, Indra's proud elephant sprayed a stream of water on his wife, Abhramuvu, and fanned her with his big ears.

24

The lord of the world and Satya went for a swim, shaded by the women of heaven, holding parasols of flowers and vines from the garden.

25

Unable to bear her heavy breasts
and the burden of her hips,
Satya moved slowly,
leaning on Krishna's shoulder.
Thrilled at the touch,
their bodies tingled with pleasure.

26

Krishna saw the heavenly river
with dark green reeds
swaying in the water.
The waves spread
like the dark hair of the river goddess,
unable to bear the scorching heat of the sun.

27

Krishna and Satya walked down the path of jeweled steps,
holding each other's hands for support. Together, they
moved close to the edge of the river, now a placid lake for
gods to play.

28

The women took off their ornaments and wore bathing
clothes of fine silk given by the *kalpa* tree.[8] Their bodies
gleamed like fresh jasmine flowers, and their long dark hair
brushed against rounded hips as they entered the heavenly
river.

29

Water struck by their heavy breasts
flowed in all directions,
but their deep belly buttons took it in.

Those with depth and dignity
also give refuge to those in distress.

30

The women lifted their hands,
revealing their breasts,
and splashed water laced with fragrant pollen
on Krishna,
like female elephants lifting their trunks,
showing their temples,[9]
and splashing water on their handsome lover.

31

The women slapped the water
like the beating of drums,
their hands dancing
to the music from their bracelets,
buzzing like bees.

32

The women swam,
showing off their skills
with faces, feet, and hands turned upward:
the lotuses of the river
suddenly seemed twice as many.

33

When they hit each other with lotuses,
they lifted their arms, showing rows of nail marks
like the love god's victory pillars
inscribed with his glorious titles.

34

With the women in the middle of the river, Krishna played a
game, tossing a ball of lotuses. The leaves stuck to his body.
He looked like Indra with a thousand eyes. After all, he's
Upendra, Indra's brother.[10]

35

Satyabhama swam in the water,
lazily holding on to her husband's shoulder,
her body moving gracefully
like a young queen of the geese
still new to the waves.

36

Even the river looked like a woman:
dark green plants, the ornaments on her hair,
flowing water, her braid coming loose,
cakravāka birds, her breasts.
She's now a woman of heaven.

37

With pearls broken from the necklaces floating around,
the sky river turned white as the Tamraparni.[11]
With the long dark hair of women swaying over it,
she was the black Yamuna.
With vermillion washed off from women's breasts,
she looked like the red river Shona.
With these women swimming in the water,
the heavenly Ganga became all the rivers of the world.

38

The women began to slide down the slopes of the rocks,
one after another,
their curly locks, nose rings, waists, breasts, and earrings
     jingling
like quivering arrows of *campaka* flowers
mounted on the love god's arched bow and shot,
one after another.

39

Krishna stayed for a while in the lotus pond of the heavenly
river and, like a proud elephant, finally came ashore with
Satya. The Apsarasas followed him, their long curly hair
damp with water fanning out, covering their hips.

40

They dried their hair,
put on fresh flowers,
wore perfume,
adorned themselves,
dressed in silken clothes from the *kalpa* tree:
they looked like arrows of the love god
tucked neatly in his quiver.

41

Krishna and Satya wore precious jewels and, followed by the
gods' women, they entered the city ruled by Indra, enemy
of demons. With unblinking eyes, the city's women perched
on balconies hoping for a glimpse.

42

The sun, eager to enjoy the water,
entered the western river along with
his wives, the evening shadows,
turning the river red
and the lotuses redder.

43

Its heat gone,
the evening turned the breasts of those women crimson
and made the golden mountain
shine with a new glow—
the day was nearing its end.

44

Kinnara couples emerged from
the caves of the golden mountain,
bathed in the heavenly river to cool themselves,
and rested in the alcoves of Indra's palace.

45

The sun sank into the western ocean
as if the snake that was evening
had lost the jewel on his hood when he was struck
hard by Garuda's wings.

46

All forms of darkness came together—
the color of Indra's rutting elephant from the east
the smoke of Agni's fire from the southeast
the skin of Yama's buffalo from the south
the sword of Nirruti from the southwest
the banner of Varuna from the west
the deer on Vayu's flag from the northwest
the skin of Kubera from the north
the neck of Ishana from the northeast—
darkness spread across the sky.

47

The moon appeared in the sky:
thief of the beauty in white lotuses caught red-handed,
life of *cakora* birds,
uncle of the love god,
source of all coolness,
shining gem on Shiva's hair,
a soft conch molded by the river above.

48

Krishna and Satya spent the night in Indra's palace, enjoying
the kingdom of love, and slept in each other's arms. Then
it was morning.

49

The sun appeared over the eastern mountain.
He's the herb that opens lotuses
    freeing them from the stings of bees trapped inside
    the night before,
the drug that brings day
    back to life after it died of darkness,
the magic that joins
    lovebirds separated by night,
the polish that brightens space
    after darkness dimmed its luster,
an oven that creates burning heat,
a boat that ferries you across the ocean of sin,
the casket holding within it the jewels, the First Words.[12]
He's all this and more.

50

Finally, it was time to steal the *pārijāta* tree. Mounted on
regal Garuda, Krishna fearlessly entered Indra's garden
along with Satyabhama.

51

"Krishna, who wields the discus,
the lord of all the gods,
has come today to take me to earth."
That's what the tree that grants all desires
thought to himself
as he danced with joy,
his branches shaking in the gentle breeze.

52

The other trees, sad
that Krishna was not taking them along,
began to weep,
shedding tears of honey.

53

The *pārijāta* rivals Krishna, for it too grants everything the
gods desire. As if jealous, Kamsa's killer uprooted the tree
with the same hand that raised Govardhana. He secured it
to Garuda's back, delighting Satya.

54

When Krishna uprooted the *pārijāta,*
the vines coiled around the tree
held on to its silken leaves,
as if trying to stop it from being taken away.
Can a wife let go of her husband?

55

The force of the wind from Garuda's wings toppled the other
trees in the garden, and they followed after the kidnapped
pārijāta. The watchmen looked at Krishna, whose mind was
intent only on stealing the tree, and blocked his path and
said:

56

"Krishna, you call yourself
the hero of the Yadavas,
is it right
to steal this tree and run off?
Indra gave it to his wife for her own use.
The bees are afraid
to smell its fragrance.
Even *they* follow her command."

57

She heard those words
and Satyabhama,
a slight smile on her face,
stopped her husband,
who was about to speak,
with a mere flick of her wrist,
fixed her slipping sari,
tucked her loosened hair,
and with fiery glances said:

58

"Listen, watchmen of Indra's garden!
Who is Shachi and who is Indra
to own this tree born from the ocean of milk?
Lakshmi and the precious gem Kaustubha
emerged with this tree,
and Vishnu took them.
If anyone should claim this tree
it is *he*.

This is not Indra's property.
Yes, I'm having my husband uproot it
and I'm taking it with me.
If your Shachi is really a hero's wife,
let her send her husband
to take it back from Krishna,
who obeys my every command."[13]

59

The gardeners heard Satya's proud words and were surprised.
They went and reported everything to the king of gods, who
was with his wife Shachi.

60

Indra was furious.
"What? Did he think it was the old *maddi* tree,
which he pulled from the pasture where his cows grazed,
just because it's also known as Indra's tree?[14]
Did Garuda not tell him about the power
of my *vajra* that never fails?"

61

He looked at Shachi. "Don't worry, I'm going right now. I'll
take back the tree and capture Satya's pride as well." He rose,
full of himself, and strode into Sudharma, his famous court.

62

Indra, his thousand eyes red, brandished his *vajra,* looked
toward Agni, Yama, Nirruti, Varuna, Vayu, Kubera, and
Ishana, and said, "Who does he think he is, this cowherd,
to take my *pārijāta* tree?"

63

The battle drum in Indra's courtyard
sounded relentlessly,
as if it were screaming in pain
from being beaten with wooden sticks over and over,
crying out to the gods:
"Don't go to battle with Krishna,
the creator, protector, and destroyer of the universe.
Don't be foolish!"

64

Suddenly,
saddled horses began to run amok,
elephants were let loose from their chains,
charioteers hoisted flags on their chariots,
and undefeated soldiers yelled proud words.
The city of Indra was chaotic like
the ocean churned by Mount Mandara.

65

Word began to spread,
and everyone started talking,
"He came saying:
'I'm your younger brother, your friend.'

He received all honors from Indra,
then stole this tree.
Krishna, nice relative he is."

66

The soldiers were confused and hurriedly began mounting their horses without even saddling them.

They repeatedly muttered, "Krishna! Krishna!" When people asked them, "Where is he?" they had no time to answer and only said, *"Pārijāta! Pārijāta!"* running around in a rush for battle.

They grabbed whatever they could find in the armory—spears, clubs, maces, bludgeons, axes—and when they picked up the wrong weapon, they fought among themselves to get the right one.

They said, "Can a human being stand up to all these gods: Indra, Agni, Yama, Nirruti, Varuna, Vayu, Kubera, and Ishana?"

They brandished their swords in the air, called loudly to their friends, laughed at those too timid to go to battle, and chased after chariots. Craving adventure, the soldiers gathered before the royal gate.

67

The elephants, still sleeping, were let loose but would not move. The mahouts tried to awaken them by force. That is how it was in the city of Indra, the god who killed the demon Namuchi.

68

Horses galloped, bent their heads low, fell on the earth, and rolled over. Although well trained, they refused to be saddled.

69

A soldier drunk with liquor from the *kalpa* tree
looked fiercely at his reflection
on an emerald wall of an alcove.
Thinking it was the enemy attacking him
he hit the wall with his sword,
and the sword broke in half.
Still, he went to battle,
broken blade in hand.

70

When his bow-string snapped for no reason,
another warrior, passionate for battle,
held the wooden part of the bow,
brandishing it like a club.

71

Yet another soldier
tried to string his bow,
but when the string wouldn't hook,
he threw it away,
picked up a sword,
and went to battle.

72

A soldier's wife tried to hold onto his feet,
but her delicate arms weren't strong enough,
nor could she say, "Don't go,"
her voice choked with tears.
She held onto him,
looking at him with loving eyes.
as he went off to battle,
dragging her along.

73

Seeking her permission,
a warrior embraced his wife,
angry for a long time
after a lovers' quarrel,
and left, happy, for battle.

74

"Just let me go to battle,
I'll bring you the golden feathers
of Garuda's wings as earrings,"
a warrior promised his wife,
who was blocking his way.
He went off, a big stick in hand.

75

Indra, Shachi's husband, mounted his chariot, which had
horses that fly at the speed of thought, Matali as its chario-
teer, and dark clouds waving like flags above. Indra, clad in
armor that warded off the arrows of demon enemies Puloma,
Vritra, Bala, and Jambha, was eager for battle.

76

Revanta, the horse trainer,
brought Ucchaishravas
to stand before Indra.
The horse's anklets stole his speed,
    like the snakes that eat the wind.
The bells were like walls to protect *devamaṇi*,
    the lucky circle of hair on his neck.[15]
The covering on his saddle looked like silver wings,
    rivaling Garuda's.
The strong gusts of wind as he sped away
    were like his anger at the theft of the *pārijāta*.
The golden dust kicked up by his hooves
    was the red moon rising at dusk.
Indra's horse was every inch divine.

77

The elephant Airavata
looked like the inner palace
of the goddess of war:
his four tusks strong and thick like pillars,
his ears like proud flags flapping overhead,
his temples, wide as walls,
dark with oozing ichor.

78

Agni came to fight
riding the royal goat.[16]
Holding weapons in all seven hands—
heavy club, sword, bow,
knife, drum, sacrificial ladle, and fan—
which doubled the splendor of his body,
he was terrifying to see.

79

The fire shooting from the weapon, Time, in his hands,
coupled with the redness of his eyes raging with anger,
sparked streaks of lightning from dark rain clouds.
Riding the supreme buffalo
that can overcome any horse,
Yama came
itching to fight.

80

They were terrifying to look at,
they could take any shape at will,
they excelled in doing cruel things—
such demons followed him as his retinue.
His elephant Kumuda, elegantly bedecked,
walked ahead.
The meat-eating god Nirruti,
riding on the shoulders of a human being,
came to fight,
shining sword in hand.

81

Demons with faces like
crocodiles, crabs, tortoises, and other animals
served him.
Holding the noose in his hand,
creating fear,
the lord of oceans, Varuna,
came to battle
seated on a chariot drawn by royal geese.

82

The fragrance from his body
gave respite to fatigued soldiers.
Strong winds kicked up by his club
moved the clouds that hit
the ears of the elephants of the directions,[17]
shaking them like fans.

Vayu came to battle
riding the deer.

83

Kubera came
with his son Nalakubara
and Manikantha, commanding the armies.
He walked along with Indra,
his shoulders shining
from the flashing brilliance
of Chandrahasa, his moon-shaped sword.

84

The redness of his anger intensifying
the fire from his third eye,
his sharp trident in hand,
atop his fighting bull bellowing fiercely,
Ishana came eagerly to battle,
accompanied by his ghoulish warriors.

85

Saying, "How dare he do this, that Krishna?"
the warriors of the city followed Indra
and the lords of the directions.[18]
Holding their weapons,
they folded their hands
and bowed to Indra,
competing with one another,
"Me first! Me first!"

86

Without a shadow of a doubt
that he would defeat Krishna,
Indra went to battle.
Three hundred and thirty million gods—
Maruts, Vasus, Vishvas, Rudras, Bhasvaras, and
    Tushitas—
marched proudly ahead,
supremely confident of victory.

87

Certain of their invincibility,
showing their equestrian skills,
their bodies encased in armor,
holding swords and other weapons,
yelling like heroes,
Gandharvas led by Chitrasena
came to battle
and met Indra at the city gate.

88

The gods' army marched, stomping on the earth, so the
golden mountain shook. Thick gold dust, fanned by whisks,
enveloped them, covering even the white umbrellas they
carried.

89

The weapons they were holding clanged,
and the noisy armies of Indra exited the city gate
like streams of the river
rushing from Shiva's wild matted hair.

90

Krishnaraya,
mountain slopes break at the sounds of your battle drums,
louder than Vishnu's churning of the milk ocean.
Archer equal to Drona, your sword is a ladder set to heaven
for enemies to climb, eager to make love to Apsarasas.
Your muscular arms relieve the burden
borne by the thousand hoods of the Primordial Snake.

91

You have the supreme title, "Strongest of Three Warriors,"[19]
you make Kondapali and Kondavidu
shake under the power of your marching armies,
you are the mountain that churns
the ocean that is the king of Kataka.

92

The dust kicked up by your horses,
which move faster than the wind,
blocks the shining sun.
Your strong armies cut through
hordes of trumpeting elephants
of your enemies.

Timmaya of the Kaushika lineage,
Singaya's son, blessed by Shiva with poetic skill,
composed this great poem, Theft of a Tree.
This is its fourth chapter.

Chapter 5

1

Krishnaraya,
you are worthy of praise,
beloved of Tirumaladevi,
protector of the world,
born in the lunar lineage, wide as the sea,
you are the tree of wishes.[1]

2

The sage to Janamejaya:

The gods' armies took strategic positions and announced aggressively,

3

"We're here, you thief of the *pārijāta*. You have no escape."
They surrounded Krishna, they threatened him, they filled the space with their lion-like roars and weapons spewing fire.

4

Krishna nonchalantly laughed at those excited armies of the gods. He seated Satya and the *pārijāta* in a safe place, put on the leather finger-guard, and removed his bow from its cover, made from Shesha's sloughed skin.

5

His brows bent in fury,
he strung his bow and twanged it,
secured the quivers on his back,
and began to shoot arrows at the armies,
one after another.

6

Krishna's arrows,
used to the blood of demons
now drank the blood of gods,
never tasted before.

7

"We are used to killing demons to protect the gods. Now we
have to kill the gods." Ashamed at this thought, the arrows
fled from the Sharnga bow, ran through the gods' bodies,
and buried their faces in the ground.

8

Invincible Garuda,
king of birds,
began to do his job:
with his wings, he pushed aside
    weapon-shards shattered by Krishna's bow,
stuck his beak, which once enjoyed
    the fragrance of the elixir of life,[2]
    into the bodies of elephants and raised them high,
flew ahead of Krishna's arrows
    and smashed the target before they got there,

held the gods' flags in his claws
    and ripped them to shreds.
He was everywhere:
above soldiers,
above horses,
above chariots,
as if more than a single bird.

9

Krishna's rain of arrows clouded the sky, and all twelve suns
lost their luster, ashamed to show their faces.[3]

10

Wounded by Krishna's arrows,
the moon's hard chest
rubbed by the firm breasts of his wives
now dripped blood.
It wasn't time for him to rise,
but the moon turned red.

11

Something amazing happened:
Kubera was cured of his disease
and lost his mace as well,
and the Rudras were freed from their aches
and lost their tridents too,
simply by reaching Krishna,
who heals all the pain of living.[4]

12

Yama and his buffalo became lighter—
　　the buffalo losing his horns,
　　the dread god his self-assurance.
Nirruti, strong as the lord of snakes, shattered his sword,
　　his arms now defanged.
His flames suddenly smothered,
　　Agni cooled to ashes.
Vayu took flight,
　　lucky to achieve such speed.
Varuna, lord of oceans,
　　was happy to hide in his depths.
Krishna's arrows, released from both hands,
reduced the lords of the directions to nothing,
sent them on their way.

13

Madhusudana bent his Sharnga bow into a circle and released
a torrent of cruel arrows with his strong arms, piercing the
Yakshas' chests, which now looked like latticed windows.

Vidyadharas lost their noses and ears when his unstoppable
whirling discus cut through them.

Krishna's Kaumodaki mace pulverized the Sadhyas' skulls.

His Nandaka sword smashed the Siddhas' limbs.

Nirjaras reeled from the tempestuous wind from Garuda's
wings, their bones badly broken.

Their armor crushed along with their courage, they leaped off their elephants and tried to crawl up Mount Meru; their chariots smashed and their charioteers killed, finding nowhere to hide, they cowered beneath the corpses of elephants; they hugged the necks of horses, which fell on top of each other when their legs were cut off; they pretended to be dead, trying not to breathe, and covered themselves with blankets that decorated horses and elephants; they dropped their weapons and ran, hair disheveled, pleading for help and looking for a way out; they looked like refugees fleeing the battleground, yet they heard Panchajanya, Krishna's conch, wherever they ran.[5]

When Jayanta, Nalakubara, and Chitrasena fell unconscious, their servants revived them with water from the celestial river in cups of golden lotus leaves and brought them safely home on stretchers.[6]

Varuna's goose threw him off and flew up into the sky, mistaking the broken white umbrellas for lotuses.

Yama's buffalo confused a pit of blood and brain for mud and wanted to bathe in it. Yama abandoned his stubborn, immovable buffalo, and ran off. With its master gone, it roamed aimlessly, huffing and puffing.

When Vayu deserted the battlefield, the buck he rides, left free, began to chase after the doe that fell from the unconscious moon.

The crescent moon on Rudra's matted hair was broken by Garuda's claws and fell off. The daughters of Betala, the ghost who roams the battleground, jumped with joy and began fighting with each other to take pieces of the moon to wear as earrings.

The battleground seemed strangely beautiful.

14

Indra, burning with fury, saw the lords of the directions fleeing the battleground and, hurling curses at them, yelled, "Come back! Don't run away!" He strung his rainbow,[7] coloring the clouds, and lifted his hands, causing fear even in the mountains,[8] and signaled the army to return.

15

The armies of the gods turned back at Indra's command, as a flowing river hits a mountain and makes a turn. They attacked Krishna, and the fight continued.

16

Krishna's arrows sped, hissing, like winged snakes and hit Indra's charioteer, broke his chariot, and hurt Indra himself. The king of the gods had to take cover behind his army.

17

Without a shred of doubt, the gods' armies riding in their chariots fought fiercely, filled with rage. Krishna, intent on stopping them, drove away the armies, with herds of stampeding elephants black as night, with his mace, bow, and discus, relishing their pain.

18

The armies of gods began to retreat, giving up their desire to fight. Driven by rage and shame, Indra, seated on his white elephant, attacked Krishna. The buzzing of bees attracted to its ichor mingled with its trumpeting sounds, adding to the fury of the attack.

19

Seeing Indra returning to fight, Krishna looked at the woman by his side and said with anger laced with humor:[9]

20

"Look at him,
Indra has returned.
The women of heaven are mocking him and
the lords of the directions,
who supported him,
lost their crowns and ran away.
He doesn't remember the pain
from my sharp weapons,
he has no shame.

21

"Watch what I'll do," said Krishna.
He strung his bow and shot an arrow
that pierced Indra's chest.
Unshaken, Indra shot fourteen arrows at Krishna

and thirty-two at Garuda.
The lords of the directions,
ashamed of themselves,
mounted their elephants once more.

22

Agni shot two arrows,
Yama three,
Nirruti four,
Varuna five,
Vayu six,
Kubera seven,
and Ishana eight.[10]
Krishna broke all of them to pieces
and hit their bodies
with arrows from his Sharnga bow.

23

How strange that two gods
both named Hari
should fight each other
with powerful arrows
used to killing demons—
all this to please their wives
who want the same tree![11]

24

Krishna famously killed the demon Mura.
Indra famously killed the demon Bala.
And here they fight each other.

Garudas, Uragas, and other gods
were eager to watch the battle,
but arrows covered the sky,
blocking their view.

25

Fierce was the battle of Krishna and Indra. Sparks from their arrows burned their feathery ends, but the arrows sped along, piercing each other, and hit their targets all at once. Suras, Siddhas, Sadhyas, and other gods watching from the sky were amazed.

26

The arrows built a canopy covering the sky, but the fire they produced burned the arrows into ashes, and the people watching were pleased.

27

"Did you forget me from the battle we had in the past?[12] Take this!" said Indra to Garuda, imprisoning him in a cage of arrows.

28

Krishna, angry, smashed the cage
with his sword Nandaka
and hit Indra's elephant.
The strong arrows shot from Krishna's hand
struck its temples
and released a stream of pearls,[13]
like the heavenly river

flowing from the steep slopes
of Snow Mountain.

29

"Krishna is comparable only to Indra.
Indra is comparable only to Krishna.
No one can rival either of them,"
praised Charanas, Siddhas, and Sadhyas,
their voices resounding in the sky.
Narada, the sage who thrives on battles,
danced with joy,
swinging his fan of peacock feathers.

30

Indra was furious and shot his weapon of Fire,
    but Krishna, Vishnu himself, absorbed it into his
    brilliance.
Indra used his weapon of Wind,
    but Vishnu took it into his breath.
Indra used his weapon of Sun,
    but it merged into Vishnu's right eye.
Indra released his weapon of Brahma,
    but it sank into Vishnu's navel.[14]
Indra's powerful weapon of Shiva
melted into the other half of Vishnu's body.[15]
Krishna holds the entire universe in him.
Indra can never win.

31

Krishna, seeing the time was right, hit Indra's bow-string
with his crescent-moon arrow. With a powerful dart, he hit
Indra's flag made of thundering rainclouds, and it fell like a
huge tree in a storm.

32

His eyebrows knotted in anger,
his face fierce,
his thousand eyes red with fury,
Indra, the king of gods,
cast aside his bow that lost its string,
slapped his shoulders,
calling Krishna for real battle,
and reached for his ultimate weapon,
the *vajra*.

33

With the weapon
that once cut the wings of the great mountains
Indra aimed at Krishna's chest,
brilliant with the Kaustubha gem,
and the worlds started shaking,
like water droplets
trembling on a lotus leaf.

34

"You think you're a hero
just because you have the name,
Lotus in the Navel?[16]
Take this!"
said Indra, standing up in his fierce form.
The gods in the sky trembled in fear,
crying "Ha! Ha!" in utter dismay,
as the king of gods hurled
the king of weapons.

35

The sky was engulfed with fire rising from the weapon's
        hundred sharp edges,
the elephants guarding the directions were terrified,
        encircled by its deafening sound,
the Chakravala mountains[17] protecting the earth shook,
        and the earth began to tremble
when Indra's weapon shot forth,
its brilliance brighter than the rays of the twelve suns.[18]

36

Krishna saw this and smiled.
He deftly moved his vehicle Garuda sideways,
glanced from the corner of his eye
at Indra's weapon with its hundred sharp edges
coming at him with the burning heat of the midday sun,
and caught it with his hand,
calloused by holding his sword Nandaka,
as if it were a lotus thrown at him in a game.

37

Vidyadharas ran with their hair disheveled,
Khacaras looked like a deserted crop after harvest,
Gandharvas scattered like betel nut smashed on a rock,
Garudas disappeared without a trace,
Kinnaras hid wherever they could,
Pannagas quickly took flight,
Siddhas ran without looking back,
the lords of directions fled in all directions,
and the sages who came to save Indra begged for help
when Krishna grabbed Indra's mighty *vajra*
easily in his hand.

38

When Krishna held his chief weapon, Indra felt disgraced, as
if his head were in Krishna's hands. Frightened and humil-
iated, Indra dismounted his elephant and fell at Krishna's
feet, begging for forgiveness and admitting his mistake.
Krishna received him kindly:

39

"Get up Indra. It's not your fault.
This woman, your sister-in-law,
asked for the tree, so I took it.
Take it back, it is your property."
Krishna handed over the weapon
and was about to give back the tree,
when Indra bowed to him
and said with a happy heart:

40

"What property?
Who am I to say it is mine?
You are the maker of everything.
The whole world is yours.
This *pārijāta* tree,
impossible for anyone to take,
will stay with you on earth
as long as you are there."
Krishna was pleased with these words
and gave Indra permission to leave.

41

Krishna kindly sent off Gandharvas, Nagas, Siddhas, and Sadhyas. He placed the tree and seated his wife on Garuda's shoulders and turned homeward, happy that his display of valor had appeased his wife and made her wish come true.

42

Recounting his battle with Indra to Satya, Krishna made ornaments of *pārijāta* flowers and adorned her body lovingly. Krishna, resting comfortably as if reclining on the ancient snake, crossed over the golden Meru Mountain.

43

After he crossed over Meru and approached Raivataka Mountain, the Yadu, Vrishni, and Bhoja kings greeted him with their armies. Krishna joyfully entered his city. Women standing on the jeweled terraces showered him with pearls and blessings.

44

When he crossed the city gate and came to the royal path,
a new fragrance began to spread, unlike anything smelled
before—the fragrance of *pārijāta* flowers.

45

When they saw the tree,
poor neighborhoods became wealthy,
plentiful with grain and gold,
stables for elephants and horses,
rows of jeweled mansions,
cows, buffaloes, chariots, and servants,
and ornaments of fine jewels,
all blossoming like lotuses in a pond.

46

Touched by the breeze from the tree,
their wrinkles magically vanished,
weak limbs became strong,
fallen teeth grew back,
shaky legs stood firm,
nails began to shine,
and hair turned black—
the old became young again.

47

Suddenly the deaf could hear,
the blind could see,
the lame could walk

when they smelled the fragrance of
pārijāta flowers.

48

Amazed to see this, Krishna climbed down from his vehicle
Garuda, the bird who ends the pride of snakes, and entered
his palace, a smile on his face.

49

He bowed to his parents, Devaki and Vasudeva, folded his
hands to his elder brother Balabhadra, paid his respects to
seniors, Brahmans, and relatives, hugged his friends, received
the bows of his children, younger brothers, ministers, and
others, affectionately greeted the people who love him, and
warmly sent off Garuda. He joined his beloved Satya, went
to her palace, and said to her with great joy, "Here is the tree.
This is what I promised you," and Satya was happy.

50

She praised her husband and then planted the tree at the
center of her garden and worshiped it every day.

51

"That's how a husband and wife should be—
like one person.
Look at them.
Krishna fought Indra, conquered him,
and brought the *pārijāta* for her,"
said her co-wives, all sixteen thousand of them,
to each other in wonder.

52

The tree grows huge,
offering shade to the entire city,
sometimes it shrinks
to the size of your thumb,
still other times it blooms
with the fragrant flowers of all sorts of trees,
it bears fruit ripened
to the color of jewels,
it takes any form you wish,
it grants you anything you desire—
the *pārijāta* tree in Satya's garden
never ceases to amaze.[19]

53

Then one day, Narada visited Satya and Krishna, who
were pleased with themselves for having everything they
wanted, praised for their nobility and power by everyone
in the world, and whose happiness was growing day by day.
Narada arrived, his body more luminous than an autumn
cloud. Satya and Krishna received him with honor. Comfortably
seated, Narada looked at Satya and said with a smile on
his face,

54

"Woman with a golden body, you're truly lucky. Indra's tree
is now in your backyard. You have surpassed not only your
co-wives but Shachi herself, queen of all three worlds.

55

"You should now perform the *puṇyaka* rite appropriate
to your supreme glory. I have seen Arundhati, Gauri, and
Shachi perform it with great attention. I shall tell you how
it goes, from start to finish.

56

"You should rise early in the morning,
take a vow of silence,
bathe in the river,
wear a fresh sari and ornaments of nine gems,
apply perfume, and adorn your hair with flowers,
bow to your father-in-law, mother-in-law,
and to your husband
and receive their approval.

57

"Free yourself from
anger, jealousy, and pride
and go to your co-wives' houses
the day before
and invite them to the celebration
with honor and respect.

58

"You should honor
ten thousand auspicious women
with sandal, camphor, perfumes,
new clothes, and ornaments.

Do this daily for a month
beginning from the ninth day of the waxing moon
of the first month of the year.

59

"You should then choose a Brahman
of good character,
who has learned his books,
with an auspicious appearance,
who knows the secrets of the *śāstras,*
was born in a good family,
has attained peace,
is compassionate at heart,
and knows the ultimate truth.
Choose him as your priest
to conclude the rite.

60

"You should give him:
elephants and horses,
beautiful women,
priceless jewels,
cows, land, and servants,
lots of grain and gold,
mercurial liquids,[20]
camphor, musk, and betel nuts,
all in plenty.

61

"Offering these things along with a fee,
you should give him Krishna, the lord of your life,
along with the *pārijāta* tree,
pouring water on the Brahman's palm.[21]
Give the Brahman whatever else he asks
and then take your husband back from him.
Perform this famous rite
attentive to every detail.

62

"You will have lots of wealth and gold,
you will have sons,
and you and your husband will live happily,
your hearts united as one,
unattainable for anyone else."

63

Narada instructed her in this famous rite. Satya listened
carefully, and her desires multiplied. She prepared herself
to perform it with her husband's consent.

64

People near and dear—
Yadus, Vrishnis, Kukuras, Bhojas, and Andhakas,
their in-laws, Bhishmaka, and the other sixteen thousand
      kings,
close relatives, Pandavas, Kauravas, and Panchalas,
Nanda and other cowherd families,
friendly kings, their relatives, and their friends—

the entire world of kings came along with their families
to attend the *puṇyaka* rite.

65

Supplies came from all over the world:
mountains, rivers, oceans, forests, islands,
all directions of the earth,
from everywhere you can think of.

66

On Krishna's command,
Vishvakarma, architect of the gods,
built on the slopes of Raivataka Mountain
the pinnacle of his skills,
an astonishing gem-studded pavilion
for gift giving.

67

The sky was crowded
    with flying chariots of the gods,
the directions shone with brilliant colors
    from precious gems on the crowns of human kings,
the sages who were invited covered the earth
    so its surface couldn't be seen,
the hoods of the Primordial Snake bearing the earth
    bent low under the weight of the people,
the entire universe was filled with sounds
of musical instruments playing in harmony.
The whole world was amazed at
the beginning of the great rite *puṇyaka*.

68

Krishna, killer of demons, and Satya took an auspicious bath,
wore new clothes, precious ornaments, and sandalwood
fragrance. At the appropriate time and with the consent of
elders, they vowed to perform the rite.[22]

69

Then Krishna, with the approval of the assembled guests,
formally requested Narada to consent to accept the gifts
prescribed by the rite.

70

Narada was bathed in fragrant water poured from
　　jeweled pots held by women in the prime of youth,
he was dressed in white silk cloth,
　　brighter than moonlight,
perfumes mixed with camphor, musk, and sandal paste
　　were applied to his body,
his thick hair was covered
　　with garlands of fragrant flowers,
he was adorned with jeweled ornaments,
and given all the honors of a king.
Krishna appointed Dhaumya and other sages as priests
and worshiped them as well.[23]

71

Heralded by music, Krishna arrived at the Gifting Pavilion
riding an elephant, followed by Pradyumna, Satyaki, and
Abhimanyu, along with Dharmaraja and other kings.

72

Satyabhama followed in a palanquin covered by a canopy
of pearls. Her mind was calm, fixed on the rite. Draupadi,
Subhadra, and the wives of the other invited kings accompa-
nied her, while auspicious older women led the procession.

73

With eyes wide as lotuses, she walked around the king of
trees that fulfills all wishes and entered the Gifting Pavilion,
followed by the wives of other sages. She worshiped Narada,
sage of the gods.

74

Rukmini, Krishna's chief queen, arrived with a false smile
on her face, thinking it was proper for her to go. She came
in a palanquin decorated with rubies, accompanied by all
sixteen thousand of Krishna's wives.

75

At that time the pavilion was louder than the ocean on a
    full moon day. You could hear all kinds of sounds:

the mooing of thousands of cows, ready to be given away,
    calling their calves

barking orders of officers busy arranging various gifts into
    separate mounds:
    gold, silver, copper, bronze, and other metals;
    precious gems like rubies, corals, sapphires, pearls,
    and emeralds;

grains like sesame, wheat, barley, rice, black gram, and
yellow gram;
household items like umbrellas, whisks, beds, fans,
and sandals all made of gold;
and vehicles such as elephants, horses, and chariots

lively conversations from the excited lords of the
directions, overjoyed to witness the festival

warning shouts of guards wielding canes, trying to make
room for queens of different lands

sounds of Vedic chants amplifying the pure voices of great
sages

praises from gods who gathered in the sky to watch the
glory of the festival

and the beating of many kinds of drums.

At that time, Narada raised his hand to stop the
commotion and said to Satyabhama,

76

"Woman with eyes wide as lotuses, now you should give away
your husband, the illustrious son of the Yadava family, along
with a flow of water. It is the conduct proper for this *punyaka*
rite. Make him consent to that."

77

With shyness and happiness in her heart,
with gentle glances of love and beauty,
Satyabhama looked at the lord of her life,
she lowered her face and said,
"Hero who conquered Madhu and Kaitabha,
did you hear what the sage said?"
Krishna replied with a smile on his lips,

78

"Woman with brows like the crescent moon,
why hesitate?
That is what the texts say.
Give me away without a second thought."
All the co-wives lowered their heads,
overcome with shyness.
Krishna's relatives, among the kings assembled there,
laughed, joking with each other.

79

Eyes racing back and forth like the eyes of a startled doe,
the woman obeyed the commands of the sage.
She tied her husband to the tree with a garland of flowers
like the net cast by the love god,
her hands jingling with golden bangles.

80

The cowherd god,
like an elephant impossible
for sages to tether in their hearts,
was easily tied to the divine tree
with a garland of flowers
by this woman with brilliant eyes.

81

"Hey, Krishna, people say
that you tied up the great demon-king Bali.
But look today, our girl tied you up
with a garland of flowers.
Don't be so sure of yourself anymore,"
said Satya's girlfriends, making fun of him.
The Pandava brothers—Dharmaraja, Bhima, and
    Arjuna—
laughed from behind, egging them on.[24]

82

At the appropriate time,
the sage Garga uttered the chants of intent,
and Satya gifted the lord of her life
along with the *pārijāta* tree
to Narada, best of sages,
pouring water over his hand and intoning:
tubhyam ahaṁ sampradade namo namaḥ.[25]

83

Then as a part of the rite, Satya donated mountains of precious stones, gold, and grain, and thousands of cows, horses, and elephants.

84

Narada, the sage who feeds on quarrels, took all the gifts, and freed Krishna from the flower garland that bound him to the tree and playfully said with a smile,

85

"You may be the god who is praised in all the texts, but your wife gave you to me. From now on, you have to do what I say."

86

"Hold this carefully. The strings are tuned," said Narada
    as he placed his vina on Krishna's strong shoulders.
"This is water from the Ganga. Don't spill it!"
    as he put his water pot in Krishna's left hand.
"This is my rosary. Be careful with it!"
    as he placed his rosary of lotus beads
    in Krishna's right hand.
"Hey, Shiva gave this to me. Hold it with care!"
    as he stuck his tiger skin under Krishna's arm.
Narada ordered him, "Go, go,"
and just as Krishna went a few feet,
he called out to him, "Come back."
Just for laughs, the great sage made Krishna,
the supreme trickster who killed Kamsa,
do his bidding.[26]

87

Krishna is the god whom
texts say is the end of the Vedas,
he's the beginning,
unborn,
eternal,
beyond all qualities,
father of the world,
knowledge itself,
imperishable and supreme.
The sage was fortunate
to treat him as his servant.
The world knows that god does
whatever his devotees desire.

88

Then Narada said to Krishna's lovely wife, "Young woman, take your beloved, who has stolen your heart. I will return him to you." Her face glowing with happiness, she gave all her ornaments to the sage in exchange.

89

The gods showered flowers from the sky as Satya took her husband back. They were pleased to see the glorious event.

90

Conducting the rite as the texts prescribe, Satya, with the sage's consent, called on all sixteen thousand co-wives including Rukmini, and gifted them golden pots filled with fresh flowers from the tree of wishes.[27]

91

Then Narada, the sage who disciplined his passions,
praised Krishna—
Govinda,
the beloved husband of Satya,
whose powers no human being can know—
in words composed with skill.

92

"You sleep on the ocean of milk,
you are as beautiful as the love god,
fulfiller of everyone's wishes,
you create wealth by your thought,
your shining pearl necklace is bright as quicksilver,
you frighten bad people.[28]

93

"You break the bodies of demons,
Lakshmi lives
inside you, the gods bow at your feet,
the eagle
is your vehicle; true form of truth,
you give peace
to all living beings, destroyer of the ego,
conqueror of all rival religions,
harmonizer of
all conflicting passions, you are the best,
Krishna.[29]

94

"You are dark like a dense sky of black clouds,
you crush evil men as an elephant destroys *sāla* trees;[30]
protector of silent sages,
you are friend to Charanas and Yakshas,
you are devoted to Shiva, who wears snakes as necklaces,
sages Nara and Narada are dear to you;
you obey goddess Earth,
you are at the beck and call of kings who follow the laws of
     Manu,
your abode has all the wealth of Indra.[31]

95

"Husband of Lakshmi, remover of the miseries
of existence, granter of boons to humans,
your eyes large as lotus leaves,
guardian of the virtuous,
demons flee from you,
protector of all sages,
you raised the earth
from the ocean.[32]

96

"You embrace the waists of gopis,
please them with your multiple forms;
indestructible one, your discus is powerful
as the hot rays of the sun,
boar that destroys the anthills of existence,
your body is dark,
sacrifices celebrate you;

I praise you, lord of the world,
your power is vast,
you hold a conch, brilliant white as the moon,
you are kind,
Radha loves you.[33]

97

"Beyond the grasp of great sages,
believe me, I won't give up
meditating on your name,
command me to live in love of your name.

98

"Your shoulders bear the marks of making love to
    Lakshmi,
your dark body shames the sapphire,
your actions worry the evil minds of demons,
you have a conch in your hand and lotus in your navel;
remover of sins,
supreme person,
your name erases the cycles of life,
Shiva is always on your mind,
your feet are tender as new leaves,
you sleep on the ocean of milk.

99

"Son of Vasudeva,
dark as rain clouds,
the goddess of wealth resides in you,
the sounds of your flute are the First Texts,

your games are known by the rasa dance you play,
even your name is praised by Indra and other gods."

100

Narada sang of him in wondrous and picturesque ways and
went away. Krishna, the lover of gopis, along with his friends,
returned to his palace.

101

He received Bhoja, Yudhishthira, Duryodhana, and the
other kings of the earth and their relatives.[34] He honored
them with gifts of clothes and jewels from the *pārijāta* tree
and sent them away.

He lived in endless happiness

102

in groves where the new rains left
    drops of water at the tips of new leaves,
    and cool breezes spread the fragrance of fresh flowers

103

in arbors near the banks of ponds
    dusted with pollen stirred up
    by the wings of bees, attracted to
    newly blossoming lotuses,

104

in caves of imaginary mountains
    studded with emerald, agate, topaz, coral,

lapis, pearl, sapphire, diamond, ruby,
and other precious stones.

105

If Rukmini were a lake, he would be the royal goose.
Satyabhama a parrot, he the cage for her to play in.
Jambhavati the night, he the moonlight.
Kalindi a lotus, he a bee.
Bhadra a peacock, he a raincloud.
Mitravinda a garden, he the spring.
Lakshana a necklace, he its pendant.
His sixteen thousand women a herd of elephants,
      he a royal bull—
that was how Krishna played,
the lord who protects the whole world.

106

Timmaya
of the Kaushika clan and Apastambha lineage
in the flawless Six Thousand Family,
son of Nandi Singana and Timmamba,
wise with learning,
nephew of the poet honored as "Cool Breeze from Malaya
      Mountain,"
feted by King Krishnaraya with palanquins and gifts of
      villages,
his mind focused on Shiva,
disciple of Aghorashivaguru,
composed this Telugu poem, Theft of a Tree, *to last as long as the sun, stars, and moon.*

107

Krishnaraya,
emperor who rules the world under one umbrella,
the finest fruit of the prayers of King Narasimha,
at festivals you give away pearls equal to your weight,
women with round breasts see you as the god of love,
the king of Karnata whose fame spreads to every horizon,
you are like a lion,
your enemies run from you like frightened elephants.

108

You are like a rising sun shining
on the nine gems of your assembly hall, named Conquest of
  the World,
you are devoted to worshiping the feet of Lakshmi's husband,
you smashed your enemy Virarudra as Indra smashed the
  mountains.

109

Your glory is equal to Indra's
gained by meditating on the feet of Shiva, Love's destroyer.
You are generous as Kubera, Kamadhenu, Karna,
  rainclouds.
You are like the gem-studded stage around which great poets
  gather.
Wise ruler, you always follow Manu,
endlessly compassionate,
your palaces resound with bees buzzing around
the temples of your fierce elephants,
inviting good fortune, Shri.[35]

Timmaya of the Kaushika lineage,
Singaya's son, blessed by Shiva with poetic skill,
composed this great poem, Theft of a Tree.
This is its fifth chapter.

Theft of a Tree *ends here.*

ABBREVIATIONS

D   Dusi Ramamurti Sastri
N   Nagapudi Kuppusvamayya

NOTES TO THE TRANSLATION

Chapter 1

1 Shri (śrī) is an auspicious syllable, and beginning with Nannaya (c. eleventh century C.E.) Telugu poets started all of their poems with this syllable. See also ch. 5, v. 109, note 38.

2 This refers to the specific ritual in a Telugu wedding ceremony in which the married couple pours grains of rice on each other's heads as a mark of auspiciousness. This practice is still commonplace in Telugu weddings today.

3 In order to end a lovers' quarrel, Vishnu places the items from his four hands—bow, discus, sword, and conch—on Lakshmi's waist, hips, hair, and neck, respectively. The verse implies that Vishnu's four objects are shaped like Lakshmi's corresponding body parts. According to the commentator Dusi (Timmana 1960: 6), this verse can be read as a template for the entire narrative of *Theft of a Tree*, in which Krishna must steal the *pārijāta* tree to appease Satyabhama's anger.

4 According to Dusi (Timmana 1960: 9), Yavana refers to Turkish troops.

5 Lakkambika is also known as Bukkambika in Peddana 2015: 1.27.

6 There is a pun here on the word *kuntala*, which means hair.

7 We do not exactly know where Manavadurga is located. Later references to this fort cite Timmana's *Theft of a Tree* as the source for Narasa's victory at Manavadurga. See Ayyangar 1919: 106–108.

8 There is a pun here on the word *madhura*, which means sweetness.

9 According to Dusi (Timmana 1960: 12), the sixteen gifts were gold, silver, copper, brass, cows, elephants, horses, dwellings, land, bull, clothes, beds, fields, shoes, servants, and food.

10 This verse references the churning of the ocean of milk by the gods and antigods, who used Mount Mandara as a churning rod.

11 Yayati had five sons: Yadu and Anu by his wife Devayana, and Puru, Druhyu, and Turvasu by his wife Sharmishta. The Sanskrit *Mahābhārata Ādiparvan* 1.7.70–80 (translated in Buitenen 1973: 171–194) includes the narrative of Yayati, who was cursed to become prematurely old. Yayati disinherited his son Yadu because Yadu refused to exchange his youth for his father's old age. Although

the name Yadu is not mentioned in ch. 1, v. 7, Yadu is the older half brother of Turvasu. In ch. 1, v. 19, the relationship with Yadu is highlighted in order to identify Krishnaraya as part of the Yadu lineage, like the god Krishna.

12   In this verse, there is a comparison between Krishna, the god, and Krishnaraya, the king. At the end of the verse, it is suggested that Krishnaraya himself is god.

13   Conventionally, the earth is carried by the cardinal elephants (*diggajālu*) and the thousand-hooded snake, Adishesha. The king who rules the country is also seen as one who carries the burden of the earth.

14   Krishnadevaraya is said to have captured Virabhadra, the son of Prataparudra, at Kondavidu. See Ayyangar 1919: 137. This event is also referenced in Krishnadevaraya's *Āmuktamālyada* 2.102 (or 2.101 in some versions of the text). According to the *Āmuktamālyada* commentator Tummapudi Kotesvara Rao (Krishnadevaraya 2001: 182), Virabhadra and his wives were imprisoned by Krishnadevaraya at Kondavidu, where they died. Historical evidence does not prove this one way or the other.

15   In tantric ritual, a man who wants a woman to fall in love with him should make snakes copulate and cover them with a white cloth. He should then use that cloth to cover the woman he desires. In this verse, the earth is perceived as a woman, the Utkala king's wife.

16   In the Mahabharata, Karna is famous for being a great giver.

17   Manu's text is the *Mānavadharmaśāstra* (Laws of Manu).

18   *Śaśikānta* or *candrakānta*, translated here as moonstone, refers to a stone that is said to melt in moonlight.

19   Narada is supposed to enjoy battle and to dance at the time of battle.

20   The poet is connecting the "tree of liberation" (*mokṣadrumamu*) with Narada's matted locks, which look like the leaf buds on that tree.

21   This verse references all of the avatars that Krishna has previously taken.

22   These two lines reference the avatars of Buddha and Kalki, who come after Krishna's incarnation. The Buddha avatar of Vishnu's ten avatars is not Gautama Buddha. Rather, this Buddha takes on the form of a beautiful man and seduces the wives of the Three Cities. Another reference to Buddha appears in ch. 3, v. 37.

23   For women, quivering on the right side of the body is considered to be inauspicious (for men, on the left).

24 This verse refers to when Satyabhama helped Krishna in his battle with the demon king Naraka. See Bammera Potana's *Śrīmadāndhra Bhāgavatamu daśamaskandamu* 10.159–176.

25 By convention, lovebird (*cakravāka*) is separated each night from its mate.

26 A husband is thought to protect his wife in seven ways, as a mother, father, husband, giver, knowledge, teacher, and god.

27 A woman would retire to her "anger chamber" when upset with her husband (comparable to the *boudoir*, "sulking-place," in eighteenth-century aristocratic France). See also *Rāmāyaṇa Ayodhyakāṇḍa* 9.15–9.20 and 9.40–9.45 (Valmiki 2005b: 82–87).

28 *Nīpa* refers to the Kadamba, an evergreen, tropical tree.

29 The sandal color stands for Krishnaraya's fame, and vermillion for his valor.

Chapter 2

1 Here, "First Words" are the Upanishads, which are perceived as women who worship at Vishnu's feet.

2 *Āmla* refers to Indian gooseberry.

3 Timmana uses a Sanskrit series compound, *bahupadadvandva*, to describe how Narada and Krishna relish the tastes of five kinds of food, i.e., foods that can be eaten, chewed, relished, sucked, and drunk, respectively.

4 Although it seems that both Satyabhama and Krishna followed Narada to the dining hall in ch. 2, v. 17, this verse indicates that Satyabhama ate her meal in her own inner palace (*antapuramuna*). In traditional settings, men and women do not eat together.

5 Verses 30–70 describe the setting sun, nightfall, and sunrise. In certain verses, Sun, Moon, Dawn, etc., are personified, while in other verses they belong to the natural world. We have capitalized these terms when they are personified in the Telugu text and have not used capitalization when the imagery invokes the natural world.

6 The gods requested the sage Agastya drink the ocean. See *Mahābhārata Vanaparvan* 3.33.101–103 (translated in Buitenen 1975: 421–424).

7 It is considered good luck if a banana plant yields its fruit toward the east. See Nagapudi (Timmana 1929: 104–105) for commentary on ch. 2, v. 42.

8 According to *Bhāgavata Purāṇa* 10.65 (translated in Bryant 2005: 280–283), Balarama calls the river Yamuna to flow toward him.

Yamuna refuses, thinking that he was drunk when he called. Balarama draws a line with his plow and forces the river to flow toward him. Balarama is red in color, wears black clothes, is always drunk, and carries a plow as his weapon.

9 *Rĕllu* is a type of wild grass in to South Asia.

10 A watch (*yāma*) is equivalent to three hours.

11 Airavana is an alternate name for Indra's elephant, Airavata.

12 The love god is said to have only five arrows. However, in a battle, warriors use thirty-two. Making love is generally described as fighting a battle, so the thirty-two arrows in this verse is considered appropriate by both commentators. See Nagapudi (Timmana 1929: 124) and Dusi (Timmana 1960: 147–148).

13 Demons called Mandehas attack the sun as he is rising. The sun saves himself by the offering of water given by Brahmans in the morning prayers.

14 This verse follows the Telugu vowel order; the consonant *ś* (sh) is combined with each of the Telugu vowels (e.g., Sharnga, Shesha, and Shiva).

15 Here the artist Time is using a cloth to paint like a brush. See Nagapudi (Timmana 1929: 129–130).

16 The young Krishna killed the demoness Putana. She came pretending to nurse him, and he sucked out her life breath.

17 *Bimba* is a scarlet, cherry-like fruit; lips are often compared to *bimba* in poetry.

18 In Telugu culture, friends snap their fingers in front of the mouth of someone who yawns.

19 There is a pun on the word *rāja* in this verse. It can mean either the king or the moon.

20 This verse refers to *dohadas*, which are: (1) the cravings of pregnant women; or (2) acts that make plants blossom when they are delayed in blooming or make them blossom out of season. This verse invokes the second meaning. *Dohada* acts vary from plant to plant; in the case of the red *gogu* (hemp) flower, the sweet sounds of women's talk make them bloom. In this verse, Dawn is personified as a woman, and the birds' morning songs are likened to Dawn's soft words. See ch. 3, v. 44 and ch. 4, vv. 9–10 for other examples of *dohadas* in this text.

21 Indra's diamond weapon is invincible, so Garuda gave it a feather from his body and escaped from it.

22 Garuda's mother, Vinata, and her co-wife Kadru engaged in a wager

that Vinata lost, which resulted in her lifelong servitude to Kadru's serpent sons. The serpents told Garuda that he and his mother would be released from servitude only if he brought to them the the elixir of life. Knowing that he must fight the gods to procure the elixir, Garuda asked his father, Kashyapa, for some food to strengthen him. His father directed him toward a tortoise and an elephant who were fighting at a nearby lake and assured his son that eating these two animals would give him the strength required to obtain the elixir. Finally, Vishnu promised that Garuda, after retrieving the elixir, would become his vehicle. See *Mahābhārata Ādiparvan* 1.5.19–26 (translated in Buitenen 1973: 77–85).

23 When the Three Cities flew in the sky, landing wherever they wanted and destroying people, Shiva fought against them. Shiva made Vishnu his arrow and Garuda the feathers of that arrow.

24 In the story of Garuda retrieving the elixir of life, he is said to have landed on a *rohiṇa* tree, or in some accounts a banyan tree, to eat the tortoise and elephant. After he landed on the tree, the branch broke, and he carried it in his mouth so as not to disturb the Valakhilya sages hanging from it. See *Mahābhārata Ādiparvan* 1.5.25–26 (translated in Buitenen 1973: 83). See also Dusi (Timmana 1960: 164–165).

25 The serpent Adishesha carries the burden of the earth.

26 Yamuna is the daughter of the sun.

27 All mountains had wings until Indra cut them off to make the mountains immobile. See also ch. 2, v. 72, note 21, which refers to Indra's *vajra* and Garuda.

28 Chenchu here refers to a hill tribe. The following verses refer to a number of divine groups, including Yakshas and Sadhyas.

29 The mark on the moon is perceived as a deer.

30 Pearls and pearl-like substances are found inside of elephants' temples, boars' tusks, bamboo stalks, and clouds, as well as inside of conch and oyster shells. The verse exhibits an ornament of speech called "picking up the last word" (*muktapadagrasta*), in which the last word of a segment is used as the first word of the next segment.

31 See ch. 2, v. 85, note 27.

32 The demon Rahu swallows the moon or the sun during an eclipse.

33 In this section, the sentences carry a double meaning (*śleṣa*).

34 *Śakra* is the hill jasmine. It is a handsome tall tree with clusters of sweet-smelling white blossoms. *Pura* is a name for the Indian

Bdellium or Indian myrrh tree. This tree is the source of an aromatic resin that is burnt as incense. The *mahila* plant is one of the Beautyberry species. It is an evergreen shrub that bears clusters of pinkish purple flowers and clusters of fruit that look like strings of pearls.

35 *Kakubha,* also called *arjuna* or *maddi,* may refer to any of the many Terminalia species found in South Asia. It is a large evergreen tree with woody drupes that are used as dice.

36 The fourfold army consists of chariots, elephants, horses, and foot soldiers.

37 In this section, the poet uses an ornament of speech called *virodhābhāsa,* in which there is an opposition in each pair, but in the semantic meaning the opposition is resolved.

38 In this poem, Gandharvas are described as having horse heads.

39 On behalf of their father, King Sagara's sons tore up the entire world in search of a sacrificial horse. In order to stop their destruction of the world, Vasudeva came in the form of the sage Kapila and burned the sons to ashes. Since they were burned by Kapila, only the heavenly waters from the Ganga could be used to perform their funerary rituals, an act achieved by their great-grandson Bhagiratha.

40 These are all things that are said to be born from the churning of the milk ocean. The wishing stone is called Chintamani.

41 *Bhañjalika, murali,* and *sudhāla* are the names of three kinds of maneuvers that Garuda displays in flight. See Dusi (Timmana 1960: 188).

Chapter 3

1 Here, in the Telugu verse, King Krishnaraya is referred to as *pañcāla,* which is one of four classifications of men found in some *Kāmaśāstra* works, along with *bhadra, datta,* and *kūcimāra.* In the Telugu text *Kāmakalānidhi* by Nelluri Shivaramakavi, *pañcāla* is described as "a man who is devoted to only one woman" (1926: 28–29). In *Kāmakalānidhi,* Rama is given as an example of *pañcāla.* See Shivaramakavi (1926: 27) and commentary by Nagapudi (Timmana 1929: 175).

2 The eight lords of the directions are: Indra, Agni, Yama, Nirruti, Varuna, Vayu, Kubera, and Ishana.

3 *Atasi* is the Indian flax plant. Also called the linseed, it is an herb with sky-blue flowers.

178

4   Chapter 3, vv. 28–38 describe the avatars of Vishnu.

5   *Ketaka* (also *mŏgali* in ch. 4, v. 16) is the fragrant screw pine. A large evergreen shrub that resembles a palm, it has strong smelling creamy yellow flowers that bloom in the monsoon.

6   Kashyapa has two wives, Aditi and Diti. Aditi's sons are the Adityas, or the gods. Diti's sons are the Daityas, or the demons.

7   In Vishnu's incarnation as Parashurama, or Rama with the Ax, he killed all royal clans with his ax.

8   Ravana took Mount Kailasa and made Shiva protect him while he was living there, which made the mountain feel humiliated. When Rama killed Ravana, the fame of Rama washed away the mountain's shame. See Dusi (Timmana 1960: 212).

9   This particular segment, called a *daṇḍaka* (garland), is a metrical form used both in long texts, such as *prabandhas* (epic poems like Timmana's that include both verse and meter), and independently. It expresses a mood of devotion and praise. Although translated here as prose, it includes a constant repetition of the same cluster of syllables. In this particular *daṇḍaka,* the meter begins with two *na-gaṇas* (three short syllables) followed by any number of *ra-gaṇas* (long syllable + short syllable + long syllable). See the introduction for a discussion of this *daṇḍaka.*

10 The terms referenced here—"chakra" and the three types of knots (*jālandhara, uḍyāṇa,* and *mūla*)—are part of hatha yogic terminology. For further discussion, see White 2012: 276–277.

11 Vishnu holds five weapons in his four arms; one weapon, the bow, is held on his shoulder.

12 The first *"Kāvu, kāvu!"* is the imperative of the Telugu verb "to protect." The second *"Kāvu, kāvu!"* is an onomatopoeic reference indicating the sound of an infant's cry.

13 *Maddi* is a kind of arjuna tree found in South Asia. Here the two *maddi* trees are the brothers Nalakubara and Manigriva. Narada cursed the brothers and turned them into trees because they failed to cover their nakedness when he happened upon them while they were playing with Apsarasas in the river. Narada gave them a reprieve, stating that they would regain their real forms when Krishna felled the trees. Here Krishna crawls with the heavy mortar between the two trees, causing the trees to fall. See *Bhāgavata Purāṇa* 10.9.22–23 and 10.10.1–43 (translated in Bryant 2005: 47–51), and Narayana Rao and Shulman (2002: 66).

14 *Guñja* (also *gurivĕnda* in ch. 3, v. 48) is the rosary pea plant. Its

glossy scarlet seeds marked with a single black spot are used as inexpensive ornaments.

15 This is from *Bhāgavata Purāṇa* 10.1.36–37 (translated in Bryant 2005: 150–154).

16 See also Bryant 2005: ch. 36, note 6.

17 Ugrasena is the father of Kamsa and the grandfather of Krishna.

18 Krishna's grandson, Aniruddha, fell in love with Bana's daughter Usha. He made love to Usha, who became pregnant. Bana learned of this and waged war against Aniruddha. In order to protect his grandson, Krishna fought with Bana, but Bana received a pledge from Shiva to protect his city. This is how Krishna came to fight against Shiva and his army, including Ganesha and Kumara. See *Bhāgavata Purāṇa* 10.2.62–63 (translated in Bryant 2005: 268–276).

19 There is an apparent contradiction in this verse, which states that Krishna accepted Aditi's invitation but then looked at Indra, who invited Krishna to Vaijayanta.

20 Indra's elephant, Airavata, and horse, Ucchaishravas, were both born from the milk ocean.

21 This refers to *santānavṛksamu*, one of the *kalpa* trees of the heavens.

22 *Mandāra* is another of the *kalpa* trees of the heavens.

23 This refers to *haricandana*, another one of the *kalpa* trees of the heavens.

24 The names used for the designs that Kubera's wife makes—conch (*śaṅkha*), lotus (*padma*), and crocodile (*makara*)—are also among the names of the nine deposits of Kubera's treasures (*navanidhi*).

25 According to Nagapudi (Timmana 1929: 218), all of the wives of the gods of the directions are mentioned except for Parvati, the wife of Ishana (a form of Shiva), suggesting that Timmana did not want Parvati to be depicted as one of the attendants of Indra.

26 For *dohadas,* see ch. 2, v. 70 and ch. 4, vv. 9–10; also see the glossary entry. The gods' women must perform specific acts to a particular tree to encourage it to blossom. Ch. 4, v. 10 provides a list of the trees and the corresponding acts that the gods' women must perform for the trees to blossom. *Kuravaka* (also *krovi* and *kŏravi* in ch. 4, vv. 9–10, respectively) is a short shrub that bears red or white flowers in spiky clusters during spring. *Kesara* (also

pogaḍa in ch. 4, v. 9) is the Ceylon Ironwood, a tropical tree with drooping leaves that are crimson and dark green. It has large white flowers with striking yellow stamens. *Kaṅkeḷi* (also called *aśoka* in ch. 4, v. 10) is a small tree with dark green leaves and clumps of orange-red flowers. *Sinduvāra* (also *vāvili* in ch. 4, v. 10) is an evergreen shrub with racemes of pale white flowers. It is often described as growing on the banks of bodies of water.

27   *Cāmanti* is the Chrysanthemum, a fragrant plant with flowers resembling small sunflowers. *Preṅkana*, the Almondette tree or Cuddappah Almond, has small green and white flowers and tiny edible nuts. *Pāṭali* (also *kaligŏṭṭu* in ch. 3, v. 51), or the Trumpet flower, is a tall tree with pink trumpet-shaped flowers that usually blossom in summer.

28   Krishna stole the clothes of gopis while they were bathing in the Yamuna river.

29   *Gŏjjega* (also *gŏjjagl* in ch. 4, v. 16) is a kind of jasmine vine or shrub with fragrant, star-shaped, white flowers. *Goraṇṭa*, or henna plant, refers to the red-flowered *kuraṇṭa* shrub. *Kaligŏṭṭu* (also *pāṭali* in ch. 3, v. 46), or the Trumpet flower, is a tall tree with pink trumpet shaped flowers that usually flower in summer.

Chapter 4

1   We differ from Nagapudi's (Timmana 1929: 233) and Dusi's (Timmana 1960: 249) interpretation of *kavitāprāvīṇyaphaṇīśa*, which they both translate as: "You are skilled in poetry like the lord of snakes."

2   For examples of the literary convention of *dohada*, see ch. 2, v. 70 and ch. 3, v. 44. *Tilaka* is a medium-sized tree with golden-red flowers. *Māmiḍi* (also called māvi in ch. 4, v. 10) is the mango tree. *Gogu,* the Indian Laburnum, is a handsome tree with bursts of odorless sulphur-yellow blossoms. *Pŏnna,* the Alexandrine Laurel, is a tropical evergreen plant with clusters of fragrant white flowers.

3   Both Nagapudi (Timmana 1929: 236–237) and Dusi (Timmana 1960: 254–254) note a distinction between the *dohada* acts as they appear in ch. 4, vv. 9–10. In the case of ch. 4, v. 9, the gods' women have to imagine various trees and perform the corresponding *dohada* acts to the *kalpa* tree. In the case of ch. 4, v. 10, the *kalpa* tree does not need the gods' women to contemplate various trees before they perform the corresponding *dohada* acts; the *dohada*

acts alone are sufficient to cause the blossoming of various flowers on the *kalpa* tree.

4   Vishnu's feet are marked by the auspicious signs of a conch and discus.

5   The meter here is *ragaḍa*, which often is used in Telugu *prabandhas* to describe women plucking flowers. Other examples include Peddana 2015: 3.84 and Ramarajabhushana 1906: 3.149. We have separated the *ragaḍa* into couplets based on the end rhyme found in the Telugu text. In his commentary on the *ragaḍa*, Nagapudi (Timmana 1929: 423) speaks disparagingly about the nature of women's speech, calling it inherently disconnected. Contrary to the commentator, we do not see this section's depicting an innate quality of women's speech; rather, the section represents overheard conversations among these women as they pick flowers.

6   *Möggali* is an aromatic plant that is commonly referred to as fragrant screw pine and is also called *ketaka* in ch. 3, v. 31. *Göjjagi* is a flowering plant and is also called *göjjega* in ch. 3, v. 51.

7   Snakes are said to eat the cool breeze or the wind as their food. For another example, see ch. 4, v. 76.

8   The original verse has *cīnipāvaḍulu*, which means undergarments made of Chinese silk.

9   Timmana here uses *kumbha* to refer to an elephant's temples and *kucakhumbha* to refer to a woman's breast, drawing a parallel between the two.

10   According to south Indian versions of the Ramayana, including Kampan's *Irāmāvatāram*, the sage Gautama cursed Indra, giving him one thousand vaginas all over his body, for making love to his wife Ahalya. When Indra begged for forgiveness, Gautama said that the vaginas would look like eyes for anyone who sees, and, therefore, Indra is known as the god of a thousand eyes. See Ramanujan 1991: 24–33.

11   The river is considered to be a source of pearls.

12   According to Nagapudi (Timmana 1929: 259), the sun is described as a form of the three Vedas in the *Ādityamantra*.

13   See the introduction for a discussion of this verse.

14   *Indradruma* (Indra's tree) is also called a *maddi* tree. Here, Indra is referring to a story from Krishna's childhood, when Krishna crawled with a mortar between two *maddi* trees and felled them. See ch. 3, v. 38, note 13 for a discussion of this narrative.

15 *Sūḍi* is a circular hair that forms on a horse's body and determines whether the horse is lucky or unlucky. *Devamaṇi* is the name of the *sūḍi* on Ucchaishravas's body.

16 Agni, god of fire, rides on a goat as his vehicle.

17 See ch 1., v. 20, note 13 for a discussion of the elephants of the directions.

18 See ch. 3, v. 3, note 2 for a list of the lords of the directions.

19 "Strongest of Three Warrlors" (*mūrurāyaragaṇḍa*) refers to three leaders: lord of horses, lord of elephants, and lord of men. The Turks were considered to have an army strong in cavalry, the Orissa kings had an army strong in elephants, and Krishnadevaraya had an army strong in soldiers.

Chapter 5

1 In this verse, the poet compares the lunar lineage of Krishnadevaraya to the *pārijāta* tree born from the ocean of milk.

2 Garuda carried the pot of elixir of life and delivered it to the snakes to free his mother from slavery. See ch. 2, v. 72, note 22.

3 According to Hindu mythology, there are twelve suns instead of just one.

4 This verse has a double meaning: Kubera's weapon, *gada,* also can mean a disease; the Rudras' weapon, *śūla,* also can mean a shooting pain in the stomach. In mythology, Kubera is described as one who suffers from a disease.

5 There is no subject for this part of the prose passage in the Telugu text. Dusi (Timmana 1960: 317) assumes it is Yakshas, Sadhyas, and Vidyadharas; Nagapudi (Timmana 1929: 289) interprets it as Yakshas, Vidyadharas, Sadhyas, Siddhas, and Nirjaras.

6 The word here is *palakagarbha,* indicating a flat surface akin to a modern stretcher.

7 In Telugu and other Indic languages, the rainbow is called Indra's bow (*indradhanus*).

8 Earlier, Indra cut off the wings of the mountains, which were forced to settle in one place. It is suggested here that when he lifted his hand, the mountains were afraid he might hit them again.

9 Timmana appears to have forgotten that in ch. 5, v. 4, Krishna put Satyabhama and the *pārijāta* tree down from Garuda's back. Here in ch. 5, v. 19, she is next to him.

10 If you count the lords of the directions, beginning clockwise with

Indra as east, and assign a corresponding number to each of the gods, the number of arrows in this verse matches the number of directions.

11 This verse is written in the voice of the poet, who is commenting on the battle.

12 See ch. 2, v. 72, note 22.

13 See ch. 2, v. 88, note 30.

14 Brahma was born from Vishnu's navel.

15 This line references Vishnu's form as Harihara, the god who is half-Vishnu and half-Shiva.

16 Here, we read Indra's use of the epithet "Lotus in the Navel" (*amboruhanābha*) as intentionally sarcastic, rather than simply as a name for Krishna.

17 The Chakravala mountains are a mythical mountain range that is said to encircle the earth.

18 This verse is composed in the infrequently used *mahāsragdhara* meter, which has four long lines. Each line is a single Sanskrit *bahuvrīhi* compound packed with harsh consonant clusters and aspirated sounds. The *mahāsragdhara* meter is suitable for expressing an earth-shaking event as described in this verse. See *Kavijanāśrayamu* 2.136 (Malliyarecana 2016).

19 This verse can be read as a metapoetic reflection of the entire *prabandha,* with the notion of fragrance substituting for melodious sound and imaginative production.

20 Mercury (*rasa*) is often mentioned in Ayurvedic materia medica (such as the *Vastuguṇa-dīpikā*) as a substance used in rejuvenating medications.

21 Pouring water on the palm is how one gives a gift to a Brahman.

22 Syntactically the verse begins with a singular subject, *dānavabhedi* ("The killer of demons"), and moves to a plural subject, *satyayunudānu* ("Satya and he"), but the verse ends with a singular finite verb. We translated it with a plural finite verb.

23 There is no subject named in ch. 5, v. 70, suggesting that the subject, Krishna, is carried over from the previous verse, v. 69. Verse 69 uses active voice, indicating that Krishna himself performed these services for Narada. We prefer to translate most of the verse in passive voice, suggesting that Krishna arranged the services for Narada, because it would be odd suggesting that Krishna himself bathed and clothed Narada. We used active voice in translating

the last two lines, in which Krishna appoints the sages Dhaumya and others as priests.

24 The eldest three Pandava brothers are related to Krishna as brothers-in-law, and therefore they can joke with him.

25 A Sanskrit utterance: "To you I give. And I bow to you." See the introduction for a discussion of this line.

26 Narada speaks to Krishna in the tone of a master speaking to his servant. This verse echoes *Harivamśa*, Appendix I.29.1531–1543.

27 Satyabhama gives her co-wives a "women's gift" (*vāyanamulu*). The term is used in Telugu only for a women's rite when women give ritually prescribed gifts to the other women who are invited to the rite.

28 Ch. 5, vv. 92–99 use *bandhakāvya*, also referred to as *citrakāvya*, a genre of poetry composed in Sanskrit, Telugu, and other vernacular Indian languages that includes a variety of patterned verses, word puzzles, and figural poems. Each line praises a different aspect of Krishna as Vishnu, but the meaning is subservient to the sound and shape of each verse. Our translation includes enjambment across lines (e.g., verses 93 and 95) to reflect the figural quality of the Telugu text. Ch. 5, v. 92 is an example of *pādabhramakamu*, in which each line can be read forward (i.e., from beginning to end) or backward (i.e., from end to beginning) and remains the same line.

29 This verse is composed in the crisscrossing pattern known as "a cow's urination" (*gomūtrikābandhamu*).

30 *Sāla* is a kind of *maddi* or arjuna tree found in South Asia.

31 This verse is in the shape of a coiled snake (*kuṇḍalināgabandhamu*). See the introduction for the figure.

32 This verse is arranged in the shape of a dagger (*chūrikābandhamu*).

33 This verse is arranged in the shape of a wheel (*cakrabandhamu*).

34 It is notable that even Duryodhana, the chief of the Kaurava clan, attended the ritual.

35 The meter here is *maṅgaḷamahāśrī*. The poem ends, as it begins, with the auspicious syllable Shri (*śrī*). See also ch. 1, v. 1, note 1.

GLOSSARY

ADISHESHA *(ādiśeṣa)* the First Snake, who bears the burden of the earth

ADITI one of the wives of the sage Kashyapa and mother of the Adityas, the gods

AGNI god of fire and one of the lords of the directions

AIRAVATA *(airāvata)* a white elephant and vehicle of the god Indra

amṛta elixir of life produced by the gods' and antigods' churning of the ocean of milk

APSARASAS celestial courtesans, also referred to as the gods' women

ARUNDHATI wife of the sage Vasishtha

BRAHMA the creator god who resides in the lotus that arises from Vishnu's navel

BRAHMAN *(brāhmaṇa)* the highest of the four social classes *(varṇa)*

cakora mythic bird fabled to subsist on moonbeams

cakravāka mythic lovebird that is separated each night from its mate; according to convention, the two birds spend the night crying in sorrow from separation

campaka the Himalayan Magnolia, a small tree with tubular flowers that may be white, yellow, or orange. According to poetic convention, bees do not go near *campaka* flowers

CHARANA *(cāraṇa)* a class of demigods

DITI one of the wives of the sage Kashyapa and mother of the Daityas, the antigods

dohada in this text, acts that make plants blossom when they are delayed in blooming or make them blossom out of season

DVARAKA *(dvāraka)* abode of Krishna on earth

GANDHARVA a class of demigods, celestial musicians

GANGA *(gaṅga)* the "sky river" that flows from the heavens to earth

GARUDA *(garuḍa)* golden eagle and vehicle of Vishnu; also can refer to a class of demigods

GAURI another name for Parvati, the consort of Shiva

INDRA king of the gods

ISHANA *(īśāna)* a form of Shiva and one of the lords of the directions

JANAMEJAYA son of King Parikshit and great-grandson of the Pandava hero Arjuna

kalpa generic name for the wish-giving tree found in Indra's garden; occasionally used in this text interchangeably with the *pārijāta* tree; see *pārijāta*

KAMSA *(kaṃsa)* uncle of Krishna

KARNA *(karṇa)* son of Kunti, the mother of the Pandavas, and the sun god; considered to be a great giver

KAUMODAKI the name of Vishnu's mace

KAUSTUBHA gem on Vishnu's chest

KIMPURUSHA (*kiṃpuruṣa*) a class of demigods

KINNARA a class of demigods

KRISHNADEVARAYA (*kṛṣṇadevarāya*) sixteenth-century Vijayanagara king to whom this text is dedicated; also referred to as Krishnaraya

KUBERA god of wealth and one of the lords of the directions

LAKSHMI (*lakṣmi*) goddess of wealth and consort of Vishnu

MANDARA name of a cosmic mountain that is used as a churning rod in the churning of the ocean of milk

MANDEHAS demons who try to prevent the sun from rising

NANDAKA the name of Vishnu's sword

NARAKA son of goddess Earth who was defeated by Krishna

NIRRUTI meat-eating god and one of the lords of the directions

PANCHAJANYA (*pāñcajanya*) the name of Vishnu's conch

PARASHURAMA (*paraśurāma*) "Rama with the Ax"; a Brahman warrior and *avatāra* of Vishnu

pārijāta the fragrant, flowering plant that can be called the coral jasmine; in this text, the *pārijāta* is described as a heavenly tree

in Indra's garden that grants all wishes; see *kalpa*

PARVATI (*pārvati*) the consort of Shiva

puṇyaka vrata rite performed by Satyabhama in which she gives the *pārijāta* tree and Krishna to the sage Narada and buys them back with gold and other forms of wealth

PUTANA (*pūtana*) demoness who tried to kill baby Krishna

RAMBHA the most beautiful of the gods' women

SARASVATI goddess of knowledge and consort of Brahma

SHARNGA (*śārṅga*) the name of Vishnu's bow

SHACHI (*śaci*) wife of Indra

SHIVA (*śiva*) the destroyer god of the Hindu traditions

SIDDHA a class of demigods

UCCHAISHRAVAS (*ucchaiśravas*) the horse of Indra

VAIJAYANTA abode of Indra in the heavens

VAISHAMPAYANA (*vaiśampāyana*) pupil of sage Vyasa and narrator of the Mahabharata as well as this text

vajra Indra's diamond weapon

VARUNA (*varuṇa*) god of the oceans and one of the lords of the directions

VASU a class of demigods

VAYU (*vāyu*) god of wind and one of the lords of the directions

VEDAS the earliest Sanskrit texts; referred to as "First Words" (*toliminukulu*) in this text

VIDYADHARA (*vidyādhara*) a class of demigods

VISHNU (*viṣṇu*) the preserver god; interchangeable with Krishna in this text

YAKSHA (*yakṣa*) a class of demigods; servants of Kubera, the god of wealth

YAMA god of death and one of the lords of the directions

BIBLIOGRAPHY

Editions

Timmana, Nandi. n.d. *Pārijātāpaharaṇamu*. Paper manuscript B. 216, D. 559. Chennai: Government Oriental Manuscript Library, C. P. Brown Collection.

Timmana, Nandi.1929. *Pārijātāpaharaṇamu*. Commentary by Nagapudi Kuppusvamayya. Chennapuri: Andhrapatrika Mudraksharashala.

Timmana, Nandi. 1960. *Pārijātāpaharaṇamu*. Commentary by Dusi Ramamurti Sastri. Madras: V. Ramaswamy Sastrulu & Sons. Original edition, 1933.

Timmana, Nandi. 2022. *Theft of a Tree*. Translated by Harshita Mruthinti Kamath and Velcheru Narayana Rao. Murty Classical Library of India 32. Cambridge, Mass.: Harvard University Press.

Other Sources

Austin, Christopher. 2013. "The Fructification of the Tale of a Tree: The Pārijātaharaṇa in the *Harivaṃśa* and Its Appendices." *Journal of the American Oriental Society* 133, 2: 249–268.

Ayyangar, S. Krishnaswami. 1919. *Sources of Vijayanagar History*. Madras: University of Madras.

Bryant, Edwin, trans. 2005. *Krishna: The Beautiful Legend of God (Śrīmad Bhāgavata Purāṇa Book X)*. London: Penguin Classics.

Buitenen, J. A. B. van, ed. and trans. 1973. *The Mahābhārata, Book 1: The Book of the Beginning*. Chicago: University of Chicago Press.

———. 1975. *The Mahābhārata. Volume 2: Book 2: The Book of the Assembly Hall; Book 3: The Book of the Forest*. Chicago: University of Chicago Press.

Dehejia, Harsha V. 2015. *Pārijāta-haraṇa: Kṛṣṇa Steals the Pārijāta*. New Delhi: D.K. Printworld.

Harivaṃśa. Vol. 1, *Critical Text*. 1969. Edited by Parashuram Lakshman Vaidya. Pune: Bhandarkar Oriental Research Institute.

Harivaṃśa. Vol. 2, *Appendices*. 1971. Edited by Parashuram Lakshman Vaidya. Pune: Bhandarkar Oriental Research Institute.

Kavikarnapura. 2008. *Pārijātāharaṇam: A Mahākāvya by Kavikarṇa-*

pūra. Darabhanga: Mithila Institute of Post-graduate Studies and Research in Sanskrit Learning.

Krishnadevaraya. 1964. *Āmuktamālyada*. Edited with commentary by Vedamu Venkataraya Sastri. Madras: Vedamu Venkataraya Sastri and Brothers.

———. 2001. *Āmuktamālyada*. Edited with commentary by Tummapudi Kotesvara Rao. Hyderabad: Malayakuta Publications.

Malliyarecana. 2016. *Kavijanāśrayamu*. With commentary by Vaidyam Venkateshvaracaryulu and S. V. Rama Rao. Hyderabad: Telangana Sahitya Akademi.

Murtakavi, Kakamani. 1894. *Pāñcālīpariṇayamu*. Rajamahendra Varamu: Vivekavardhani Mudraksharashala.

Narayana Rao, Velcheru. 2003. *Hibiscus on the Lake: Twentieth-Century Telugu Poetry from India*. Madison: University of Wisconsin Press.

Narayana Rao, Velcheru, and David Shulman. 1998. *A Poem at the Right Moment: Remembered Verses from Premodern South India*. Berkeley: University of California Press.

———. 2002. *Classical Telugu Poetry*. Berkeley: University of California Press.

Peddana, Allasani. 2015. *The Story of Manu*. Translated by Velcheru Narayana Rao and David Shulman. Murty Classical Library of India 4. Cambridge, Mass.: Harvard University Press.

Potana, Bammera. 1992. *Śrīmadāndhra Bhāgavatamu daśamaskandamu*. Commentary by Palavarti Nageswara Sastry. Kakinada: Sri Saraswati Dharmika Vidya Trust.

Ramanujan, A. K. 1991. "Three Hundred *Rāmāyaṇas*: Five Examples and Three Thoughts on Translation." In *Many Rāmāyaṇas: The Diversity of a Narrative Tradition in South Asia*," ed. Paula Richman. Berkeley: University of California Press, pp. 22–49.

Ramarajabhushana. 1906. *Vasucaritramu*. Chennapatnamu: Sri Venkateshvara Mudraksharashala.

Shivaramakavi, Nelluri. 1926. *Kāmakaḷānidhi anu śṛṅgāra*. Madras: Ganti Suryanarayana Sastry.

Smith, William L. 2007. "Assam: Shankaradeva's *Parijata Harana Nata*." In *Krishna: A Source Book*, ed. Edwin Bryant. New York: Oxford University Press, pp. 163–186.

Śrīviṣṇu Mahāpurāṇamu. 2008. Hyderabad: Sri Venkateshvara Arshabharati Trust.

Suranna, Pingali. 2002. *The Sound of the Kiss, or The Story That Must*

Never Be Told. Translated by Velcheru Narayana Rao and David Shulman. New York: Columbia University Press.

Tirupati Rao, Cannapragada. 2000. *Pārijātāharaṇamu: Jagannātha vijayamuto tulanātmakānuśīlanamu*. Bangalore: Author.

Valmiki. 2005a. *Ramáyana I: Boyhood*. Translated by Robert Goldman. Clay Sanskrit Library. New York: New York University Press and JJC Foundation.

———. 2005b. *Ramáyana II: Ayódhya*. Translated by Sheldon Pollock. Clay Sanskrit Library. New York: New York University Press and JJC Foundation.

White, David Gordon. 2012. *The Alchemical Body: Siddha Traditions in Medieval India*. Chicago: University of Chicago Press.